Heck's Pictorial Archive of Art and Architecture

EDITED BY

J. G. HECK

DOVER PUBLICATIONS, INC.

NEW YORK

Bibliographical Note

This Dover edition, first published in 1994, contains the complete sections "Architecture," "Mythology and Religious Rites" and "The Fine Arts" (116 plates) and the accompanying descriptive contents of the plates from the *Iconographic Encyclopædia of Science, Literature, and Art. Systematically Arranged by J. G. Heck. Translated from the German, with Additions, and Edited by Spencer F. Baird, A.M., M.D., Professor of Natural Sciences in Dickinson College, Carlisle, PA. Illustrated by Five Hundred Steel Plates, Containing Upwards of Twelve Thousand Engravings,* originally published by Rudolph Garrigue, Publisher, New York, in 1851. The table of contents has been slightly rearranged for this edition.

Library of Congress Cataloging-in-Publication Data

Heck, J. G. (Johann Georg), d. 1857.
  [Bilder Atlas zum Conversations Lexicon. English. Selections]
  Heck's pictorial archive of art and architecture / edited by J.G. Heck.
      p.   cm. — (Dover pictorial archive series)
  A selection of engravings from the Iconographic encyclopaedia of science, literature, and art (New York, 1851), which was a translation of Heck's Bilder Atlas zum Conversations Lexicon.
  ISBN 0-486-28254-6 (pbk.)
  1. Engraving—19th century. 2. Architecture—Pictorial works. 3. Mythology—Pictorial works. 4. Art—Pictorial works. I. Title. II. Title: Pictorial archive of art and architecture. III. Series.
NE486. H4313 1994
741.6—dc20   94-25895
                                                                  CIP

Manufactured in the United States of America
Dover Publications, Inc., 31 East 2nd Street, Mineola, N.Y. 11501

Contents

ARCHITECTURE

PLATE 1.

Fig. 1. Rock temple of Mavalipuram
" 2. Pagoda at Chalembaram
" 3. Pagoda at Tretshengur
" 4. Pagoda near Benares
" 5. Interior of the temple of Indra
" 6, 7. Grotto temples

PLATE 2.

Fig. 1. Temple of Kailasa near Ellora
" 2. Temple of Indra Sabah at Ellora
" 3. Interior of the grotto temple on the island of Elephanta
" 4. Interior of the temple of Wisua Karmah at Ellora

PLATE 3.

Figs. 1, 2. Sculptures from Nineveh
" 3-11. Fragments from Persepolis
" 12. Tomb of Nakshirustam
" 13-15. Hindoo pillars

PLATE 4.

Fig. 1. Temple of Antæopolis
" 2. Theatre in Antinoe
" 3. Ruins of Apollinopolis Magna
" 4. Temple of Carnak
" 5a. Temple of Tentyra
" 5b. Temple at Latopolis
" 6. Temple on the island of Philæ
" 7. Rock-cut tombs of Silsilis
" 8. Entrance to the temple of Typhon at Denderah

PLATE 5.

Figs. 1-6. Temple of Apollinopolis Magna
" 7. Plan of the Palace of Carnak
" 8-11. Details from the same
" 12. Catacombs at Thebes
" 13, 14. Catacombs of Alexandria

PLATE 6.

Fig. 1. Pyramid in Lake Mœris
" 2. Pyramids of Gizeh
" 3. Section of a pyramid at Memphis
" 4. Pyramid at Assur in Nubia
" 5. Colossi at Thebes
" 6. The Sphinx of Gizeh
" 7. Hall of the palace at Carnak
" 8. Entrance into the palace of Luxor
" 9. Propylæa on the island of Philæ

PLATE 7.

Figs. 1-24. Illustrating general considerations on architecture

PLATE 8.

Fig. 1. The Acropolis of Tiryns
" 2. Section of the same
" 3, 4. The Grottoes of Corneto
" 5. The Gate of the Lions at Mycenæ
" 6. Section through the same
" 7. Entrance of the Treasury of Atreus at Mycenæ
" 8. Section of the same
" 9-11. Plan and sections of the Giganteja on the Island of Gozzo

PLATE 9.

Fig. 1. View of ancient Athens
" 2. Western front of the Parthenon
" 3. The temple of Theseus
" 4. The Tower of the Winds
" 5. The Choragian monument of Lysicrates
" 6. Temple of Segesta in Sicily

PLATE 10.

Figs. 1, 2. Temple of Jupiter at Olympia
" 3-5. Temple of Theseus
" 6. Eastern front of the Parthenon
" 7. Plan of the Parthenon
" 8, 9. Temple of Minerva Polias, &c.
" 10-12. The Odeon in Athens
" 13, 14. Doric portico
" 15. Temple on the Ilissus
" 16. The temple of Diana in Eleusis

Fig. 17. Temple of Cybele in Sardis
" 18, 19. Temple of Concordia in Agrigentum
" 20, 21. Temple at Pæstum
" 22, 23. Temple at Euxomus in Ionia
" 24-27. Temples at Pæstum

PLATE 11.

Fig. 1. The Acropolis of Athens
" 2. Temple of Jupiter Olympius in Athens, elevation
" 3. Ditto, plan
" 4. Ditto, section
" 5. Temple of Minerva Polias, Erechtheus, and the Hall of the Nymph Pandrosos in Athens (restored view)
" 6. Longitudinal section of the Parthenon in Athens
" 7, 8. Temple of Castor and Pollux in Rome
" 9-12. Temple of Faustina in Rome
" 13. Plan of the temple of Cybele in Sardis
" 14. Plan of the temple of Concordia in Agrigentum
" 15. Plan of the temple of Juno in Agrigentum
" 16, 17. Plans of Doric temples in Selinuntiæ
" 18. Plan of the temple of Ceres in Pæstum
" 19. Plan of the temple of Minerva in Sunium
" 20. Plan of the temple of Apollo at Bassæ

PLATE 12.

Figs. 1, 2. Temple of Diana at Ephesus
" 3, 4. Temple of Apollo at Miletus
" 5, 6. Temple of Bacchus at Teos
" 7, 8. Temple of Diana in Magnesia
" 9. Ruins of the temple of Neptune at Pæstum
" 10, 11. Temple of Jupiter at Selinuntiæ
" 12. Temple of the Sun in Palmyra
" 13, 14. Temple of Nemesis at Rhamnus
" 15, 16. Temple of Portumnus at Ostia,
" 17. Temple of Jupiter in Rome

PLATE 13.

Fig. 1. Ruins of Baalbec
" 2. Plan of the temple of the Sun at Baalbec
" 3. Plan of the temple of Jupiter at Baalbec
" 4, 5. Temple of Concordia in Rome,
" 6. Plan of the temple of the Sun in Palmyra
" 7. Plan of the temple of Mars in Rome
" 8. Plan of the temple of Portumnus in Ostia
" 9. Plan of the temple of Serapis in Pozzuoli
" 10. Plan of the temple of Augustus in Pompeii
" 11. Plan of the Rotunda on the Via Prænestina in Rome
" 12. Plan of the temple of Theseus in Athens
" 13. Plan of the temple of Jupiter in Ægina
" 14, 15. Portico of Metellus
" 16, 17. Forum of Nerva
" 18-22ab. Mausoleum at Halicarnassus

PLATE 14.

Fig. 1. The Forum Romanum
" 2. Amphitheatre of Flavius
" 3. Half ground plan of the Coliseum
" 4. Section of the Amphitheatre at Verona
" 5. Section of the Amphitheatre at Nismes

PLATE 15.

Figs. 1, 2. Temple of Neptune in Pæstum
" 3-5. Temple of Jupiter at Olympia
" 6, 7. Temple of Jupiter Capitolinus in Rome
" 8. Temple of the Sun in Rome
" 9. Plan of the Temple of Quirinus in Rome
" 10, 11. Maison Quarrée in Nismes
" 12, 13. Temple of Honor and Virtue in Rome
" 14. Plan of the temple of Ceres at Pæstum
" 15. Plan of the temple of Jupiter in Forli
" 16. Plan of the temple of Pietas in Rome
" 17. Plan of the temple of Janus in Rome
" 18. Plan of the temple of Spes in Rome
" 19. Plan of the temple of Minerva in Syracuse

PLATE 16.

Figs. 1-6. Temple of Venus and Rome in Rome
" 7, 8. Temple of Fortuna Virilis in Rome
" 9-12. Temple of Vesta in Tivoli
" 13. Ruins of the temple of Jupiter at Baalbec
" 14. Plan of the temple of Jupiter Olympius in Athens
" 15. Plan of the temple of the Sun in Rome
" 16. Plan of the temple of the Sun in Baalbec
" 17. Plan of the temple of Jupiter Nemæus near Corinth
" 18. Plan of the temple of Minerva at Priene
" 19. Plan of the temple of Diana at Eleusis
" 20. Plan of the temple of Jupiter at Ostia
" 21. Plan of the temple of Minerva in Assisi
" 22. Plan of a temple at Palmyra
" 23. Plan of the temple of Nemesis at Rhamnus
" 24. Plan of the temple of Hercules at Cori
" 25. Plan of the temple of Augustus at Pola
" 26. Plan of a temple at Selinuntiæ
" 27. Plan of a temple at Palmyra
" 28. Plan of the temple of Fortune in Pompeii
" 29. Plan of the chapel of Mercury in Pompeii
" 30. Plan of the chapel of Isis in Pompeii
" 31. Plan of the temple of Æsculapius in Pompeii
" 32. Plan of the temple of Nike Apteros in Athens
" 33. Plan of the temple of Themis at Rhamnus
" 34. Plan of a temple at Selinuntiæ
" 35. Plan of the temple of Diana in Eleusis
" 36. Plan of an Ionic temple at Athens,
" 37. Plan of the temple of Jupiter at Pompeii
" 38. Plan of a temple of the Sybil in Tivoli

PLATE 17.

Figs. 1-3. The Odeon of Pericles at Athens
" 4-7. The Pantheon in Rome
" 8-13. The island of the Tiber, with its temple and bridges
" 14. The bridge of Æmilius in Rome
" 15. The bridge of Senators in Rome
" 16ab. Triumphal arch at Xaintes

Fig. 17*ab*. The arch of Gabius in Verona
  " 18*ab*. Trajan's triumphal arch at Ancona
  " 19*ab*. Trajan's triumphal arch at Beneventum
  " 20. Triumphal arch of Septimius Severus in Rome
  " 21. Constantine's triumphal arch in Rome
  " 22*ab*. Pedestals at Palmyra
  " 23*ab*. The tomb of the Horatii near Albano

PLATE 18.

Figs. 1–7. Hadrian's mausoleum in Rome,
  " 8, 9. The Trophæon of Augustus near Torbia
  " 10. Sepulchre of Septimius Severus in Rome
  " 11, 12. Trajan's triumphal arch in Beneventum
  " 13, 14. Constantine's triumphal arch in Rome
  " 15, 16. Triumphal arch of Marius in Orange
  " 17, 18. Triumphal arch of Titus in Rome
  " 19*ab*. Gate of Verona
  " 20, 21. Triumphal arch of Augustus at Pola
  " 22, 23. Gate of Mylasa
  " 24–30. Trajan's column in Rome
  " 31–36. Column of Marcus Aurelius in Rome

PLATE 19.

Fig. 1. Doric capital from Pæstum
  " 2. Ditto, from Delos
  " 3. Ditto, from Pæstum
  " 4. Ditto, from Albano
  " 5. Ditto, from Rome
  " 6*ab*. Ionic capitals from Athens
  " 7, 8. Ditto, from Rome
  " 9. Corinthian capital from Athens
  " 10. Ditto, from Athens
  " 11. Ditto, from Rome
  " 12. Ditto, from Rome
  " 13. Ditto, from Rome
  " 14. Composite capital from Albano
  " 15. Ditto, from Rome
  " 16, 17. Attic base from Athens
  " 18. Corinthian base from Athens
  " 19. Ditto, from Tivoli
  " 20. Ditto, from Rome
  " 21. Ditto, from Rome
  " 22. Ornamented base from Nismes
  " 23. Ditto, from Rome
  " 24. Crowning flower from Athens
  " 25, 26. Ornamented shafts from Rome
  " 27. Architrave soffit from Rome
  " 28. Ditto, from Rome
  " 29. Frieze from Palmyra
  " 30. A Persian
  " 31. A Caryatide
  " 32, 33. Terminal statues (Hermæ)
  " 34–38. Antefixæ

PLATE 20.

Fig. 1. Tuscan order
  " 2. Doric order
  " 3. Ionic order
  " 4. Corinthian order
  " 5. Composite order
  " 6. Tuscan column arrangement with arches
  " 7. Tuscan pedestal
  " 8. Doric entablature
  " 9. Details of the Doric order
  " 10–13. Illustrating the reduction and torsion of columns
  " 14. Scotia of the Attic base
  " 14*a*. A Corinthian door
  " 15. Doric door
  " 16–19. Balusters

PLATE 21.

Fig. 1. Tuscan column arrangement,
  " 2. Doric entablature
  " 3. Doric column arrangement
  " 4. Ionic capital
  " 5. Ionic column arrangement
  " 6. Corinthian capital
  " 7. Corinthian column arrangement
  " 8. Composite capital
  " 9. Arrangement of Composite columns,

PLATE 22.

Fig. 1. Tuscan capital and entablature
  " 2. Doric base and pedestal

Fig. 3. Doric capital and entablature
  " 4. Ionic base and pedestal
  " 5. Ionic capital and entablature
  " 6. Corinthian base and pedestal
  " 7. Corinthian capital and entablature
  " 8. Composite base and pedestal
  " 9. Composite capital and entablature

PLATE 23.

Fig. 1. Tuscan arcade
  " 2, 3. Doric arcades
  " 4, 5. Ionic arcades
  " 6, 7. Corinthian arcades
  " 8, 9. Composite arcades

PLATE 24.

Fig. 1. Men-hir in Bretagne
  " 2. Half Dolmen of Kerland
  " 3. Dolmen of Trie
  " 4. Double Dolmen of the Island of Anglesea
  " 5. Trilith at St. Nazaire
  " 6. Druid altar near Cleder
  " 7. Rocking stone near West Hoadley
  " 8. Rocking stone of Perros-Guyrech
  " 9. Covered way in Morbihan
  " 10. Dolmen of Locmariaquer
  " 11. Grotto near Esse
  " 12. Grotto des Fées near Tours
  " 13, 14. The witches' grotto near Saumur
  " 15. Mound at Salisbury
  " 16. Galleries in a mound near Pornic,
  " 17. Section of a mound in the Orkneys
  " 18. Pierced stone near Duneau and Gallic Tomb
  " 19. Cromlech from the Orkneys

PLATE 25.

Figs. 1–11. Details of Chinese houses
  " 12. Chinese ceiling
  " 13. Chinese window
  " 14, 15. Chinese roofs
  " 16. Dwelling of a mandarin
  " 17. Porcelain tower near Pekin
  " 18, 19. Pagoda at Ho-nang
  " 20. Entrance to the temple of Confucius in Tsing-hai

PLATE 26.

Fig. 1. Bridge in the district of Tlascala
  " 2. Temple at Xochicalco
  " 3. Pyramid of Teotihuacan
  " 4. The house of the ruler in Yucatan
  " 5*ab*. Details from the same
  " 6. Pyramid of Tuzapan
  " 7. Pyramid of Papantla
  " 8. Fragment from the front of the Temple of the Two Serpents in Uxmal

PLATE 27.

Fig. 1. Plan of St. Marcelline's church in Rome
  " 2. Plan of St. Martin's church in Tours
  " 3. Plan of the church of Parenzo
  " 4. Plan of St. Paul's before the walls of Rome
  " 5. Plan of St. Peter's basilica in Rome
  " 6. Plan of the basilica Santa Maria Maggiore in Rome
  " 7. Plan of the church of the Holy Cross, Jerusalem
  " 8–13. The basilica St. Lorenzo in Rome
  " 14. Church of St. Agnes near Rome
  " 15. Basilica of St. Stephen in Rome
  " 16. Romanesque basilica
  " 17. St. Clement's basilica in Rome
  " 18. Rear view of a basilica
  " 19, 20. Ciborium and choir of St. Clement's in Rome
  " 21–24. Baptisteries
  " 25–27. Baptismal fonts
  " 28. Baptistery in Cividale
  " 29. Baptistery in the basilica of St. Agnes in Rome
  " 30. Cloister in St. Paul's basilica before Rome

PLATE 28.

Fig. 1. Panhagia Nicodimo in Athens
  " 2. Church of Samara in Greece
  " 3, 4. St. Sophia's in Constantinople

Figs. 5–12. The church of Theotokus in Constantinople
  " 13, 14. Details of the Panhagia Nicodimo
  " 15. St. John's Church in Pavia
  " 16. Church in Trani
  " 17. St. Castor's church in Coblentz
  " 18. Mausoleum of Theodoric in Ravenna
  " 19. Capital from the Turkish baths in Constantinople

PLATE 29.

Figs. 1–8. St. Vital's church in Ravenna
  " 9–17. The Catholicon in Athens
  " 18. Plan of St. Sophia's in Constantinople
  " 19. Plan of the mosque Achmed in Constantinople

PLATE 30.

Figs. 1, 2. St. Peter's basilica in Rome
  " 3–5. Cathedral of Pisa
  " 6, 7. St. Mark's church in Venice
  " 8. Court of the mosque of Osman in Constantinople
  " 9*ab*. Cathedral of Bonn
  " 10, 11. Ruins of a Latin basilica near Athens
  " 12. Plan of the church of Navarino
  " 13. Side portal of St. Nicodemus's church in Athens
  " 14. Choir of St. Theotokus's church in Constantinople
  " 15–23. Details from Byzantine edifices
  " 24. Plan of the church of St. Agnes in Rome
  " 25. Plan of the basilica in Tyre

PLATE 31.

Fig. 1. Interior of the mosque of Cordova
  " 2. Interior of the hall Maksourah in the mosque of Cordova
  " 3. Interior of the chapel Zancaron in Seville
  " 4. Entrance of the villa El Generalife in Granada
  " 5. Court of the mosque El Moyed in Cairo

PLATE 32.

Fig. 1. The Court of the Lions in Alhambra
  " 2–12. Details from Alhambra
  " 13. The Golden Hall in Alhambra
  " 14. The Hall of the Two Sisters
  " 15. The mosque at Cordova, longitudinal section
  " 16–25. Details from the same
  " 26. Mosque of Ebn Touloun in Cairo longitudinal section
  " 27–33. Details from the same

PLATE 33.

Fig. 1. Plan of the mosque at Cordova
  " 2–4. Details from the same
  " 5. Plan of the mosque of Ebn Touloun at Cairo
  " 6. Court in the same
  " 7. Plan of the mosque of El-Moyed in Cairo
  " 8. Mausoleum at Bedjapur
  " 9. Kutub Minar near Delhi
  " 10. The Antler Tower in Ispahan
  " 11–20. The abbey of Lorsch
  " 21–26. Basilica St. Saba at Rome

PLATE 34.

Figs. 1–39. Details illustrating the architecture of the Middle Ages
  " 40. The cathedral of Cologne as it is to be

PLATE 35.

Fig. 1. Plan of the church St. Germain de Prés
  " 2. Cross-arms of a transept
  " 3. Portal of Notre Dame la Grand in Poitiers
  " 4–15. Details illustrating the architecture of the Middle Ages
  " 16, 17. The minster of Freyburg

PLATE 36.

Figs. 1–41. Details illustrating the architecture of the Middle Ages
  " 42. The minster of Strasburg

iv

PLATE 37.

Figs. 1–22. Details illustrating the architecture of the Middle Ages
" 23. The church of St. Michael and St. Gudula in Brussels
" 24. The cathedral of Antwerp
" 25. Interior of St. Stephen's church in Vienna

PLATE 38.

Figs. 1–19. Details illustrating the architecture of the Middle Ages
" 20. The minster at York
" 21. Interior of the cathedral of Milan
" 22. The cathedral of Burgos

PLATE 39.

Figs. 1–44. Details illustrating the architecture of the Middle Ages
" 45. The cathedral of Rouen

PLATE 40.

Fig. 1. Plan of Notre Dame in Paris
" 2. Plan of the cathedral at Milan
" 3–39. Details illustrating the architecture of the Middle Ages
" 40. Interior of Notre Dame in Paris

PLATE 41.

Figs. 1–12. Details from the cathedral of Cologne
" 13, 14. Cathedral of Magdeburg
" 15. Interior of the Collegiate church in Manchester
" 16. Interior of the church of St. Simon at Palermo
" 17. Interior of Melrose abbey
" 18. Crypt under the abbey of St. Denis,

PLATE 42.

Fig. 1. The church of St. Zacharias in Venice
" 2–5. The church of Notre Dame in Vetheuil
" 6–14. Church near the charter-house near Pavia
" 15–18. The royal palace in Venice
" 19. Portal of the Ecole des Beaux Arts in Paris
" 20. Triumphal arch of Alphonso I. in Naples

PLATE 43.

Figs. 1–3. Church of the Redeemer in Venice
" 4–16. Church of St. Francis in Perugia
" 17. Plan of the church of St. Zacharias in Venice
" 18, 19. Monument of the Doge Vendramini in Venice
" 20–22. Monument of Louis XII. in St. Denis
" 23. Capital from the triumphal arch of Alfonso I. in Naples

PLATE 44.

Figs. 1–4. St. Peter's in Rome

PLATE 45.

Figs. 1, 2. The church Della Superga in Turin
" 3, 4. The church of the Assumption in Genoa
" 5. The basilica in Vicenza
" 6. The church of Santa Maria del Fiore in Florence
" 7–9. The church San Pietro in Montorio in Rome
" 10. The church delle Figlie in Venice
" 11. The church of Trevignano

PLATE 46.

Fig. 1. Interior of St. Magdalene's church in Paris
" 2. The church of Notre Dame de Lorette in Paris
" 3, 4. The church of St. Gervais and St. Protais in Paris
" 5. The church of St. Paul and St. Louis in Paris
" 6, 7. The church of Mary Magdalene at Bridgenorth

Fig. 8. All Saints church in Munich
" 9. The basilica St. Boniface in Munich
" 10. The church of San Giorgio Maggiore in Venice
" 11. The church of St. Francesco de la Vigna in Venice
" 12. The church of San Pietro in Montorio in Rome
" 13, 14. Chapel at Fresnes
" 15. Plan of the basilica Bibiana in Rome
" 16. Plan of the church of St. Agnes in Rome
" 17. Plan of the basilica Julia in Rome
" 18. Plan of the church St. Cosmo e Damiano
" 19, 20. Church Madonna degli Angeli in Rome
" 21, 22. The church of St. Cyriacus in Ancona

PLATE 47.

Figs. 1–6. The Hotel des Invalides in Paris
" 7, 8. St. Isaac's church in St. Petersburg
" 9–11. The church of the Sorbonne in Paris
" 12–14. The church of the Assumption in Paris

PLATE 48.

Figs. 1, 2. St. Magdalene's church in Paris
" 3–5. The Pantheon in Paris
" 6. Plan of Notre Dame de Lorette in Paris
" 7, 8. The Garrison church at Potsdam
" 9. The church of St. Ignatius in Rome
" 10, 11. The church of San Carlo alle Quattro Fontane in Rome
" 12. The bell tower of Palermo

PLATE 49.

Figs. 1–3. St. Paul's church in London
" 4, 5. Church of St. Sulpice in Paris
" 6. Plan of Santa Maria del Fiore in Florence
" 7. Interior of the church of All Saints in Munich
" 8. Interior of the church in Faubourg Au in Munich

PLATE 50.

Fig. 1. Interior of the Invalides' church in Paris
" 2. Church of St. Louis in Munich
" 3. Werder church in Berlin
" 4. The chapel of St. Ferdinand at Sablonville
" 5. The church Santa Maria della Vittoria in Rome
" 6, 7. The church della Consolazione in Todi
" 8. Ground plan of a church in the form of a Latin cross
" 9. Plan of the church San Andrea in Mantua
" 10–12. The chapel of the Knights of Malta in St. Petersburg
" 13. The clock tower in Venice

PLATE 51.

Figs. 1–4. The palace of Caserta near Naples
" 5. Court of the Palazzo Saoli in Genoa
" 6. Plan of the palace of Laeken
" 7. Plan of the country seat of the duke of Argyle in Scotland
" 8–13. Markets

PLATE 52.

Figs. 1, 2. The Louvre in Paris
" 3. The papal Cancelleria in Rome
" 4. The papal palace in Rome
" 5. The Palazzo Paolo in Rome
" 6. The Palazzo Sora in Rome
" 7. The Palazzo Sacchetti in Rome
" 8. The Villa Medici in Rome
" 9. The Palazzo Giraud in Rome
" 10a–c. The Casa Silvestri in Rome

Fig. 11. Ground plan of an antique Roman building

PLATE 53.

Fig. 1. The palace of the Tuileries in Paris
" 2, 3. The navy department in Paris
" 4. The Luxembourg palace in Paris
" 5. The palace of Laeken
" 6. Plan of the Glyptothek in Munich
" 7–9. The column of the Place Vendôme in Paris
" 10ab, 11. The column of July in Paris
" 12, 13. The bell tower in Rome

PLATE 54.

Fig. 1. The palace of Versailles
" 2. The battle gallery in the same
" 3. The Palazzo Doria Tursi in Genoa
" 4. The Fontana Paolina in Rome
" 5. The fountain of Marius
" 6–9. Doors from Roman palaces

PLATE 55.

Figs. 1, 2. The Walhalla at Ratisbon
" 3ab. Candelabra from the same
" 4–6. The royal residence in Amsterdam
" 7. The city hall at Maestricht
" 8, 9. The town hall in Neuenburg

PLATE 56.

Fig. 1. The Capitol at Washington
" 2. The Glyptothek in Munich
" 3. The edifice for exhibitions in Munich
" 4. The Exchange in New York
" 5–7. The Exchange in Paris
" 8, 9. Plans of the Exchange in Ghent
" 10. The University of Ghent
" 11. The Exchange in London

PLATE 57.

Fig. 1. The triumphal arch in Paris
" 2, 3. The Paris observatory
" 4. The theatre at Dresden
" 5, 6. The theatre in St. Petersburg
" 7. St. Charles theatre in New Orleans
" 8. The Custom-house in New York
" 9. Plan of the Palazzo del Te in Mantua
" 10–12. Casino in Liège
" 13. The museum in Cassel
" 14. Old Exchange in Amsterdam
" 15ab. Plans of caravansaries
" 16ab, 17. Watchhouses
" 18. Plan of the prison in Aix

PLATE 58.

Figs. 1–4. Grain hall in Paris
" 5–7. Market of St. Germain in Paris
" 8. The market at Pavia
" 9, 10. The Magdalene market in Paris
" 11. Plan of the market in Pavia
" 12, 13. The Almeidan at Ispahan

PLATE 59.

Figs. 1–14. The prison at Halle
" 15. Plan of the prison of Newgate in London
" 16–18. Plans of Prisons in Ghent Milan, and Amsterdam

PLATE 60.

Figs. 1, 2. Bridge over the Rialto in Venice
" 3–6. Bridge at Ispahan
" 7. Bridge of Gignac
" 8–10. Bridges at Paris
" 11. Waterloo bridge in London
" 12. Bridge of St. Maizence
" 13. Bridge of Kösen
" 14. Bridge of Zwetau
" 15. Bridge over the Taff
" 16. Bridge over the Melfa
" 17. Bridge of the Ticino
" 18. Bridge near Lyons
" 19, 20. Chinese bridges
" 21. Bridge of Toledo
" 22. The bridge of Colebrookdale

V

MYTHOLOGY AND RELIGIOUS RITES

PLATE 1.

Fig. 1a. Vishnu the Creator
" 1b. Brahm wrapped in the Maya
" 2. The Maya as Bhavani
" 3. Brahma, the creative power
" 4. Birth of Brahma
" 5. Siva, the destroying power
" 6. The Trimurti
" 7. The Lingam
" 8. The Hindoo symbol of wisdom
" 9. The figure Om or Aum
" 10. The Hindoo symbol of creation
" 11. Pracriti
" 12. The tortoise supporting the world
" 13. The seven celestial spheres
" 14. Siva Mahadeva
" 15. Parvati
" 16. Lakshmi or Sri
" 17. Siva as Rudra
" 18. Vishnu as man-lion
" 19. Surya, the god of the sun
" 20. Camadeva or Camos
" 21. Ganges, Jamuna, and Saraswadi
" 22. The giant Garuda
" 23. The giant Ravana
" 24. Buddhistic altar-piece
" 25–28. Buddhistic temple implements

PLATE 2.

Fig. 1. The Trimurti
" 2. Vishnu and Siva
" 3. Vishnu as a fish
" 4. Vishnu as a tortoise
" 5. Vishnu as a boar
" 6. Vishnu as a dwarf
" 7. Vishnu as Parasu Rama
" 8. Siva
" 9. Vishnu
" 10. Vishnu as Krishna
" 11. The nymphs of the Milk Sea
" 12. Vishnu as Kaninki or Katki
" 13. Siva as Hermaphrodite
" 14. Siva on the giant Muyelagin
" 15. Brahma and Saravadi
" 16. Buddha
" 17. Buddha-Surya
" 18. The Hindoo solar system
" 19. Mythic camel
" 20. Hindoo penitents
" 21–24. Hindoo sacrificial utensils
" 25–30. Mongolian idols

PLATE 3.

Figs. 1–5. Hindoo idols
" 6. Vishnu on the giant Garuda
" 7. Indian idol of Astrachan
" 8. Buddha
" 9. A Brahmin
" 10–12. Hindoo ascetics
" 13–20. Idols of Lamaism
" 21. Mongolian Lama
" 22. Tartar Lama
" 23. Funeral of the Dalai Lama

PLATE 4.

Fig. 1. Allegorical pillar from Barolli
" 2. Chinese god of immortality
" 3, 4. Chinese idols
" 5. Worship at Honan
" 6. Chinese bonzes
" 7–13. Japanese idols
" 14, 15. Japanese house gods
" 16. Temple of Nitsirin at Honrensi
" 17. Temple at Foocoosaizi
" 18–32. Buddhistic temple implements
" 33–36. Buddhistic votive tablets

PLATE 5.

Fig. 1. Worship of Fo in Canton
" 2, 3. Japanese idols
" 4. Temple of Miroc in Japan
" 5–10. Japanese idols
" 11. Chapel of the Cami at Givon
" 12, 13. The two Inari
" 14–17. The four Camini
" 18–36. Japanese temple utensils
" 37, 38. Japanese monks
" 39, 40. Buddhistic priests
" 41. Blind monk of Japan
" 42. Japanese nun and lay sister

PLATE 6.

Figs. 1–3. Japanese idols
" 4. Chief priest of the Tensjû

Fig. 5. Priest of the same
" 6. High priest of Japan
" 7, 8. Buddhistic priests
" 9. Chinese procession
" 10. Chinese fanatic
" 11. Japanese procession
" 12–15. Japanese temple utensils
" 16, 17. Necklaces of the chief priest
    of the Tensjû
" 18–23. Javanese idols

PLATE 7.

Figs. 1, 2. Persian processions
" 3. Persian Magi
" 4. Median high priest and Feruer
" 5. Persian fire worship and Feruer
" 6. Worship of the sun
" 7, 8. The priest kings
" 9. Sacrifice by Mithras
" 10, 11. Mythic animals
" 12ab. Persian coin
" 13. The celebration of the Darun
" 14. Idols of Afghanistan
" 15–17. Abraxas Gems

PLATE 8.

Fig. 1. Egyptian symbol of the sun
" 2. The All-seeing Eye
" 3–5. Sacred ships
" 6. Egyptian Amun
" 7. Nubian Amun
" 8. Kneph Mendes or Pan
" 9. Athor with the dove
" 10. Isis upon a lotus
" 11. Statue of Isis
" 12. Isis as a cow
" 13. Isis as a star
" 14. Isis nursing Osiris
" 15. Osiris upon a cow
" 16. Osiris with the serpent
" 17. Amun, Isis, and Osiris
" 18. Hermes as Ibis
" 19. Horus
" 20. The bull Apis
" 21. Typhon
" 22. Ailures
" 23. Serapis as the sun
" 24. Serapis and the seven planets
" 25. Harpocrates
" 26ab. Sacred jugs
" 27a–c. Egyptian family idols
" 28. The Sistrum
" 29. The sacred camel
" 30. The Egyptian zodiac
" 31. Priests and priestesses of Isis

PLATE 9.

Fig. 1. Kneph
" 2. Isis nursing Osiris
" 3. Isis nursing Horus
" 4. Osiris as a lion
" 5. Osiris as a bull
" 6. Anubis, Hermes, or Thot
" 7. Anubis and Isis
" 8. Anubis, Canop, and Horus
" 9. The wolf
" 10. The tribunal of the dead
" 11–14. Head-dresses of Egyptian
    idols
" 15, 16. Sacred jugs
" 17–19. Egyptian family idols
" 20, 21. Egyptian mythic animals
" 22. A sphinx
" 23. The Sistrum
" 24–28. Sacred vessels
" 29. Mystic procession
" 30, 31. Abraxas Gems

PLATE 10.

Fig. 1. Head of Isis
" 2. Isis Pharia
" 3, 4. Statues of Isis
" 5, 6. Serapis and Isis
" 7. Statue of Serapis
" 8. Serapis on his throne
" 9. Isis nursing Horus
" 10, 11. Statues of Osiris
" 12, 13. Statues of Anubis
" 14. Statue of Harpocrates
" 15. Harpocrates on a ram
" 16. The Nile
" 17. The Nile key
" 18. Kneph as Agathodemon
" 19–22. Votive hands
" 23, 24. Sphinxes

Fig. 25. The flower of the lotus
" 26–31. Egyptian priests
" 32–34. Egyptian priestesses
" 35. Sacrifice to Isis

PLATE 11.

Fig. 1. Assyrian sacrifice
" 2. Syrian idol
" 3. The goddess Astarte
" 4. Phœnician Deities,
" 5. Phœnician procession of the gods
" 6. Odin, Thor, Freyr, Tyr, and
    Loke
" 7–10. Odin
" 11ab. Norwegian idol
" 12. Ziselbog
" 13. Ipabog
" 14, 15. Slavonic idols
" 16. Nehalennia
" 17, 18. Runic stones
" 19. Runic calendar
" 20. Chinese worship

PLATE 12.

Fig. 1. Frigga
" 2. Braga
" 3. Idunna
" 4. Freya
" 5. Heimdall
" 6. The tree Yggdrasill and the
    Norns
" 7. The Valkyræ
" 8. Triglav
" 9. Svantevit
" 10. Radegast
" 11. Prove
" 12. Siebog
" 13. Shvaixtix
" 14. Nirthus or Hertha
" 15. Flyntz
" 16. Magusanus
" 17. Alemanic idol
" 18. Germanic religious ceremony
" 19. Venus Anadyomene
" 20. The Gallic Isis

PLATE 13.

Fig. 1. Odin the supreme
" 2. Thor the thunderer
" 3. Freyr, god of the sun
" 4. Freya with her maids
" 5. Njord, god of winds
" 6. Tyr, god of battle fields
" 7. Hermode the messenger
" 8. Aske and Emla, the first human
    beings
" 9. Radegast
" 10. Sieba, goddess of love
" 11. Podaga
" 12ab. Perkunust
" 13. Nemisa
" 14a. Sarmatian idol
" 14b. Silesian idol
" 15, 16. Northern idols
" 17, 18. Gallic Jupiter
" 19. Gallic Vulcan
" 20. Gallic Mercury
" 21. Hercules Saxanus
" 22. Gallic Diana
" 23. Mercury, Abelio, Vulcan, Ceres,
    and Minerva
" 24, 25. Druid and Druidess
" 26. Annual search for the mistletoe

PLATE 14.

Figs. 1–7. Mexican idols
" 8. Fragment of Aztek writing
" 9ab. Mexican priestess
" 10. The Mexican year
" 11. The Mexican almanac
" 12. Mexican altar top
" 13. Mexican sacrifice
" 14–19. Idols of Guatemala
" 20. Altar with idols
" 21–24. Sacrificial vessels of Guate-
    mala
" 25–28. Idols of Yucatan
" 29. Sacrificial vase from Yucatan
" 30, 31. Abraxas Gems

PLATE 15.

Figs. 1, 2. Statues of Janus
" 2ab. Heads of Janus
" 3. Saturnus
" 4. Opis or Ops

Fig. 5. Jupiter as Deus pater
" 6, 7. Hera
" 8. Hestia
" 9. Vesta
" 10. Diana
" 11. Apollo
" 12. Tages
" 13. Mars the advancing
" 14. Bellona
" 15 Hermes
" 16. Ancharia
" 17. Aphrodite (Venus)
" 18. Vertumnus
" 19. Pomona
" 20. Voltumna
" 21ab. Fortuna
" 22ab. Vejovis
" 23. Asclepios (Æsculapius)
" 24. Tyrrhenian Heracles
" 24ab. Sacred coin
" 25. The shield dance of the Salii
" 26ab. Demeter (Ceres)
" 27ab. Demeter and Zeus

PLATE 16.

Fig. 1. Faunus
" 2. Nemesis
" 3. Proserpine
" 4. The genius of death
" 5, 6. Two heroes
" 7-9. Lares
" 10. Æon
" 11, 12. Cronos
" 13. Cronos and Rhea
" 14. Rhea
" 15. Atys
" 16ab. Attributes of Atys
" 17. The goat Amalthea
" 18. Jupiter Axur
" 19. Zeus Ammon
" 20. The Olympian Zeus
" 21. Zeus the Supreme
" 22. Zeus with the eagle
" 23. Hera suckling Ares
" 24. Bonus Eventus
" 25. Ceres Catagusa
" 26. Diana Lucifera
" 27-33ab. Grecian sacrificial vessels
" 34. The Augures

PLATE 17.

Fig. 1. Nux or Night
" 2. Cœlus
" 3. Rhea
" 4. Jupiter Axur
" 5. Zeus Hellenios
" 6. Jupiter receiving the homage of
        the gods
" 7, 8. Zeus as warrior
" 9. Pelasgian Zeus
" 10. Zeus carrying off Europa
" 11. Birth of Athene (Minerva)
" 12. Jupiter Conservator
" 13. Pelasgian Hera
" 14-17. Juno
" 18-21. Ares (Mars)
" 22. Mars Pacificus
" 23. Victoria (Nike)
" 24. Ganymede
" 25. Hebe
" 26. Apollo and Daphne
" 27. Sibylla
" 28. Apollo's raven
" 29. A sacrificial knife
" 30. The Delphian oracle

PLATE 18.

Fig. 1. Zeus
" 2. Zeus conquering the Titans
" 3. Europa on the bull
" 4. Zeus on the centaur
" 5. Ares and Aphrodite
" 6-8. Genii of Mars
" 9. Nymph of Artemis
" 10. The Dioscuri
" 11. Poseidon, Amphitrite, and Eros
" 12. Bacchanalian genii
" 13. Dionysos (Bacchus)
" 14. Apollo
" 15. Ariadne
" 16. Demeter (Ceres)
" 17-24. Roman sacrificial implements
" 25. The assembly of the gods

PLATE 19.

Fig. 1. The twelve planet gods
" 2. Zeus, Hermes, and Aphrodite
" 3. Pallas Athene
" 4. Ceres (Demeter)
" 5. The muse Erato

Figs. 6, 7. Flora
" 8. Fortuna
" 9. A naiad
" 10. Genii
" 11. The Seasons
" 12. Tritons
" 13. Bacchanalia
" 14. Priestess of Bacchus
" 15, 16. Priestesses of Ceres
" 17, 18. Grecian priest and priestess
" 19, 20. Altars
" 21-47. Sacrificial utensils

PLATE 20.

Fig. 1. Argos guarding Io
" 2. Leda and the swan
" 3, 4. The Dioscuri
" 5. Leto (Latona)
" 6. Lunus
" 7. Apollo and Marsyas
" 8. Aurora
" 9. Artemis Locheia
" 10. Diana Lucifera
" 11. Artemis Soleia
" 12. Juno Sospita
" 13. Helios
" 14. Artemis (Diana)
" 15. Artemis and her nymphs
" 15. Mountain nymphs
" 17. Niobe
" 18. Amphion
" 19. Hermes the messenger
" 20. Hermes Agonios
" 21. Zeus with the eagle
" 22. Europa and the bull
" 23 The Panathenæan festival at
        Athens

PLATE 21.

Fig. 1. Artemis of Ephesus
" 2. Artemis Tauropolos
" 3. Artemis Selene
" 4. Hebe
" 5. Iris
" 6. Death of the children of Niobe
" 7. Nereus
" 8. Palæmon
" 9. Nereid
" 10. Taras
" 11. Poseidon
" 12. Poseidon and Pallas Athene
" 13. Hippocamp
" 14. River god and naiad
" 15ab. Nilus (the Nile)
" 16ab. Tibris (the Tiber)
" 17-19. Sirens
" 20. Artemis and Orion
" 21. Mænade
" 22. Hermes (Mercury)

PLATE 22.

Fig. 1. Hylas carried off by nymphs
" 2. Nereids
" 3. A Triton
" 4. Pelasgian Poseidon
" 5, 6. Statues of Poseidon
" 7, 7a. Neptune
" 8. Hippocamp
" 9. Melicertes (Palæmon)
" 10. Thetis
" 11. Hebe
" 12-15. The winds
" 16. Boreas bearing off Oreithyia
" 17. Hades (Pluto)
" 18ab. Proserpine (Persephone)
" 19. Sacrifice to Neptune

PLATE 23.

Fig. 1. Hades (Pluto)
" 2. Zeus Ammon
" 3. Hades (Pluto)
" 4. Poseidon and Amymone
" 5ab. Nemesis
" 6. Hypnos (Sleep)
" 7. Thanatos (Death)
" 8, 9. Hypnos (Sleep)
" 10. The genius of sleep
" 11, 12. Persephone (Proserpine)
" 13. Hecate
" 14. Erinnyes or Eumenides
" 15. Prometheus
" 16. Pandora
" 17. The Dreams
" 18. Demeter and Triptolemus
" 19. Dionysos nursed by nymphs
" 20. Triumph of Poseidon and Amphi-
        trite
" 21, 22. Tritons

PLATE 24.

Fig. 1. Pelasgian Demeter
" 2. Bust of Demeter
" 3. Ceres
" 4. Persephone
" 5. Procession of Dionysos and Ari-
        adne
" 6. Triptolemus
" 7. Birth of Dionysos
" 8. Leucothea
" 9. The sacred lion
" 10ab. The sacred serpent
" 11. Dionysus and Faunus
" 12, 13. Dionysos
" 14. Ariadne
" 15. Indian Dionysos
" 16. Pan and Olympos
" 17ab. Pan and the Panic
" 18. Silenos
" 19. Hygeia
" 20. Hephæstos (Vulcan)
" 21. Telesphorus
" 22, 23. Hermes (Mercury)
" 24. Charon
" 25. Sisyphos, Lapithæ, and Tantalos

PLATE 25.

Fig. 1. Faunus and a Bacchante
" 2, 3. Pan
" 4, 5. Dionysos
" 6. Dionysos of Naxos
" 7. The Dionysian mysteries
" 8. Apollo and Marsyas
" 9. Marsyas and Olympos
" 10-12. Silenos
" 13. Priapos
" 14-18. Heracles
" 19a. Persephone
" 19b. Dionysos Zagreus
" 20. Hephæstos (Vulcan)
" 21. Mount Parnassos

PLATE 26.

Fig. 1. The nine Muses
" 2. The muse Calliope
" 3. The muse Clio, .
" 4. The muse Polyhymnia
" 5. The muse Euterpe
" 6ab. The muse Urania
" 7. The muse Thalia
" 8. Mnemosyne
" 9a. Flora
" 9b. Vestal virgin
" 10a. Aurora
" 10b. Medusa
" 11. Apollo and the Hours
" 12. Dionysos as god of the sun

PLATE 27.

Fig. 1. Artemis (Diana)
" 2. Hermes (Mercury)
" 3. A herma
" 4. Hermes the Eloquent
" 5. Hermes with the tortoise
" 6. Vesta
" 7-14. Pallas Athene (Minerva)
" 15. The Delphian Apollo
" 16. Antinous
" 17-25a. Aphrodite (Venus)
" 25b. Mars and Ilia
" 26. Aphrodite as goddess of matri-
        mony
" 27. Mars the Avenger
" 28. Athene, Asclepios, and Hygeia
" 29. Asclepios and Hygeia
" 30. Venus Victrix
" 31. Birth of Aphrodite

PLATE 28.

Figs. 1-4. Apollo
" 5. Dionysos and Apollo
" 6. Bust of Athene (Minerva)
" 7-12. Hermes (Mercury)
" 13. Silenos
" 14-18. Aphrodite (Venus)
" 19-21. The Graces
" 22. Hermaphrodites
" 23. Hymen
" 24. Asclepios
" 25. Melicertes (Palæmon)
" 26. The sacred bull of Dionysos
" 27. Sacrifice to Mars

PLATE 29.

Fig. 1. Ariadne
" 2. Dionysian orgies
" 3-6. Eros (Amor)
" 7-10. Amor and Psyche
" 11. Statue of Psyche
" 12. The Graces
" 13. The Hours
" 14. Fides

Fig. 15. Pax
" 16. Pietas
" 17. Pudor or Pudicitia
" 18. Concordia
" 19. Bonus Eventus
" 20. Spes
" 21. Astræa
" 22. A centaur
" 23. Sacrifice in Rome

PLATE 30.

Fig. 1. Roman pontifex maximus

Fig. 2. Roman augur
" 3. Guardian of the Sibylline books
" 4. Priest of Jupiter
" 5. Vestal virgin
" 6. Victimarius
" 7. The Suovetaurilia
" 8. Sacrificial tripod
" 9. Sacrificial horn
" 10. Gorgons
" 11, 12. Perseus
" 13ab. Medusa
" 14. Charybdis

Fig. 15. Scylla
" 16. The nymph Circe
" 17. Minotaur
" 18ab. Sphinxes
" 19. A centaur
" 20. Œdipous slaying the sphinx
" 21–23. Giants
" 24. Allegorical represen'tion of Atlas
" 25, 26. Bellerophon
" 27, 28. Amazons
" 29. Pygmies
" 30, 31. Pallor, Pavor

THE FINE ARTS

PLATE 1.

Fig. 1. Bas-relief from the ruins of Persepolis
" 2. Trimurti, from the temple of
Elephanta
" 3. Bas-relief from Ellora
" 4. Bas-relief from Kenneri
" 5. Bust from Ægina
" 6. Mask from Selinuntiæ
" 7, 8. Etruscan bas-reliefs
" 9–11. Grecian sculptures of the se-
cond period
" 12. Bas-relief from Selinuntiæ
" 13, 14. Bas-reliefs from Xanthus

PLATE 2.

Figs. 1–9. Egyptian statues
" 10. Façade of the temple of Hathor
at Ipsambul
" 11, 12. Phœnician grave-stones
" 13. Numidian half-bust
" 14. Statue of Lakshmi from Bengalore
" 15. Statue from Isura
" 16–19. Persian sculptures

PLATE 3.

Fig. 1. Hercules's combat with Antæus
" 2. Aphrodite and Ares (Venus and
Mars)
" 3. The reclining Hermaphrodite
" 4. Pallas, in the Villa Albani
" 5. Pallas with the serpent
" 6. The Farnese Flora
" 7. The wounded Amazon of Ctesi-
laus
" 8. The dancing Hours
" 9. Fragment of the frieze of the
Parthenon
" 10. Fragment from the Capitoline
Museum
" 11. Bas-relief from a tripod-stand in
Dresden
" 12–17. Grecian portrait-busts
" 18–20. Grecian animal heads
" 21. The Gonzaga cameo
" 22–26. Grecian coins

PLATE 4.

Fig. 1. Phidias's statue of Pallas in the
Parthenon in Athens
" 2. The Medicean Venus
" 3. The Venus of Melos
" 4. The Venus of the Dresden Museum
" 5. The Venus Victrix from Capua
" 6. The Capitoline Venus
" 7. Diana the Huntress in Paris
" 8. Statue of Sallustia Barbara Ur-
bana with Eros, in Rome
" 9. Statue of Julia Soæmis in Rome
" 10. Sleep as a boy, in Dresden

PLATE 5.

Fig. 1, 2. The Farnese Hercules
" 3. The Torso Belvedere
" 4. The Borghese Gladiator
" 5. The Dying Gladiator
" 6. The Pallas from Velletri
" 7. Cupid and Psyche
" 8 Venus crouching in the bath
" 9. Statue of Adonis
" 10. Statue of Dionysus, in Paris
" 11. Statue of Bacchus, in Dresden
" 12. Statue of Cincinnatus in Paris
" 13. Boy extracting a thorn from his
foot, in Rome

PLATE 6.

Fig. 1. Statue of Antinous of Belvedere
" 2. The Apollo of Belvedere
" 3. Statue of a Faun
" 4. Statue of Germanicus, from the
15th century
" 5. Hercules with the boy Telephus
on his arm, in Rome
" 6. Boy wrestling with a goose
" 7. Laocoön, in the Vatican
" 8. Statue of Meleager, in Rome

PLATE 7.

Fig. 1. Pietas Militaris, bas-relief in
Rome
" 2. The restoration of the dead to
life, bas-relief in the Vatican
" 3. Statue of a bishop, by Agostino
and Angelo de Senis
" 4. Shrine of St. Peter the Martyr
by Giovanni Balducci
" 5–8. Four Caryatides from this
shrine
" 9. Bust from a fountain at Siena, by
Jacopo della Quercia
" 10. Bust of an apostle, by Andrea
Verocchio
" 11. St. John the Baptist, by Donatello
" 12. St. George, by Donatello
" 13. Holy Virgin, by Giovanni da Pisa
" 14. Apollo and Daphne, by Lorenzo
Bernini
" 15. The Angel of the Annunciation
by Francesco Mocchi
" 16. Perseus, by Benvenuto Cellini
" 17. Mercury, by Giovanni da Bo-
logna
" 18. Bacchus and a Satyr, by Michael
Angelo
" 19. Moses, by Michael Angelo
" 20. Morning and Evening, by Michael
Angelo

PLATE 8.

Fig. 1. The Three Graces with the Urn,
by Germain Pilot
" 2. The Fettered Slave, by Michael
Angelo
" 3. The Penitent Magdalene, by Canova
" 4. The Dancing Girl, by Canova
" 5. Statue of Jason, by Thorwaldsen
" 6. Statue of Apollo, by Thorwaldsen
" 7. Statue of Cincinnatus, by Chaudet
" 8. Dancing Neapolitan, by Duret
" 9. Statue of Spartacus, by Fogatier
" 10. The Maid of Orleans, by the
Duchess Marie of Orleans

PLATE 9.

Fig. 1. Statue of Hebe, by Canova
" 2. Cupid and Psyche, by Canova
" 3. The Three Graces, by Canova
" 4. Statue of Venus, by Thorwaldsen
" 5. The Three Graces, by Thorwaldsen
" 6. Achilles and Briseis, bas-relief by
Thorwaldsen
" 7–11. Fragments from the Procession of Alexander, bas-relief by Thorwaldsen

PLATE 10.

Fig. 1. Statue of Admiral Duquesne, by
Roguier

Fig. 2. Statue of Bayard, by Montour
" 3. Statue of Du Gueselin, by Bridan
" 4. Statue of the great Condé, by
Jean David
" 5. Statue of Mozart, by Schwanthaler
" 5ab. Bas-reliefs from the pedestal of
the last-named monument,
by Schwanthaler
" 6. Statue of Margrave Frederick, by
Schwanthaler
" 7. Ino with the boy Bacchus, by
Dumont
" 8. Leda and the Swan, by Seurre
jeune
" 9. Statue of Bavaria, by Rauch
" 10. Statue of Felicitas publica, by
Rauch
" 11. Monument to Marshal Saxe, by
Pigalle
" 12. Monument to Robert Burns in
Edinburgh

PLATE 11.

Fig. 1. Statue of Otto the Illustrious, by
Schwanthaler
" 2. Statue of Ludwig the Bavarian
by Schwanthaler
" 3. Statue of Gutenberg, by Jean
David
" 4. Statue of Gutenberg, by Thorwaldsen
" 5, 6. Bas-reliefs from the pedestal of
the last-named monument
by Thorwaldsen
" 7. Statue of Schiller, by Thorwaldsen
" 8, 9. Bas-reliefs from the pedestal of
the last-named monument,
by Thorwaldsen
" 10. Statue of General Kleber, by Ph.
Gross
" 11. Monument to the Duchess of
Saxe-Teschen, by Canova
" 12. The Death of Epaminondas, bas-
relief by Jean David
" 13. Bellona, bas-relief by Chinard
" 14. Monument to Dugald Stewart in
Edinburgh

PLATE 12.

Figs. 1, 2. Egyptian paintings
" 3–7. Etruscan vase-paintings
" 8, 9. Wall-paintings from Pompeii
" 10. Monochrome from Herculaneum,
" 11. Achilles and Briseis, from Pompeii
" 12. Achilles at Scyros, from Pompeii
" 13, 14. Wall-paintings from the baths
of Titus

PLATE 13.

Figs. 1–4. Etruscan vase-paintings
" 5. Theseus, wall-painting from Herculaneum
" 6. Narcissus, wall-painting from
Herculaneum
" 7. The Aldobrandini wedding
" 8. Fresco painting from the villa
Pamfili
" 9. The Pythian Apollo
" 10. The Delphian Apollo
" 11, 12. Nymphs, from the Baths of
Constantine
" 13, 14. Amorettes, from the same
" 15. Ceiling from the sepulchre of the
Naso family
" 16. Masks, mosaic in the Vatican

Fig. 17. Doves, mosaic in the Capitoline Museum
" 18. Relief-mosaic in Rome
" 19–22. Mosaic pavement

PLATE 14.

Figs. 1–3. Grecian vase-paintings
" 4. Wall-painting from the sepulchre of the Naso family
" 5ab. Miniature paintings of the 8th century
" 6. Mosaic from the Villa Albani
" 7. Mosaic from St. John's in the Lateran
" 8. Fragment from Trajan's column
" 9. Mosaic from Cosmedino
" 10. Mosaic from St. John's in the Lateran
" 11. Mosaic from Florence
" 12. Mosaic from St. Peter's in Rome

PLATE 15.

Fig. 1. School of Athens, by Raphael
" 2. Madonna and Child, by Leonardo da Vinci
" 3. Ecce Homo, by Ludovico Cardi
" 4. St. Mark, by Fra Bartolomeo
" 5. St. Francis, by Guido Reni
" 6. The Entombment of Christ, by Caravaggio
" 7. Mary Magdalen and St. Francis of Assisi by the body of Christ, by Annibale Caracci
" 8. Joseph and Potiphar's wife, by Carlo Cignani
" 9. Praying Madonna, by Sassoferrato
" 10. Madonna, by Guido Reni
" 11. St. John the Baptist, by Guido Reni
" 12. Galathea, by Ludovico Caracci
" 13. Pluto, by Agostino Caracci

PLATE 16.

Fig. 1. St. Cecilia, by Raphael
" 2. Madonna and Child, by Raphael
" 3, 4. Fresco paintings by Raphael
" 5. The Distribution of the Holy Rosaries, by Carlo Maratti
" 6. Venus and Vulcan, by Giulio Romano
" 7. Madonna, by Annibale Caracci
" 8. Descent from the Cross, by Andrea del Sarto
" 9. Polyhymnia and Erato, by Pietro da Cortona
" 10. Euterpe and Urania, by Pietro da Cortona

PLATE 17.

Figs. 1ab, 2ab. Fresco paintings, by Raphael
" 3. Raphael's portrait, by himself
" 4. The Adulteress before Christ, by Tintoretto

Fig. 5. The Dying Magdalen, by Rustichino
" 6. Holy Family, by Francesco Albano
" 7. Charity, by Andrea del Sarto
" 8. Madonna, by Murillo
" 9. Vandyk's portrait, by himself
" 10. Passage of the Granicus, by Lebrun

PLATE 18.

Fig. 1. Madonna and the Fathers of the Church, by Raphael
" 2. The Virgin Mary, by Fra Bartolomeo
" 3. Christ crowned with thorns, by Titian
" 4. Andromeda, by Francesco Furini
" 5. Offering brought to Æsculapius, by Guérin
" 6. Guido Reni's portrait, by himself,
" 7. Assumption of St. Mary, by Rubens
" 8. Portrait of Rubens, by himself
" 9. The Adoration of the Shepherds by Van der Werff
" 10. Youth with the Drinking-cup
" 11. Guitar-player, by Netscher
" 12. The Adoration of the Magi
" 13. Endymion, by Girodet-Trioson
" 14. Belisarius, by François Pascal Gérard

PLATE 19.

Illustrations of the Theory of the Art of Drawing.

Figs. 1–12. The eye
" 13–15. The nose
" 16–19. The mouth
" 20–27. The ear
" 28–31. The feet
" 32–39. The hands
" 40–45. Pictorial perspective

PLATE 20.

Illustrations of the Theory of the Art of Drawing.

Figs. 1–10. The head
" 11–14. The entire body
" 15, 16. Artistical Anatomy
" 17–21. The hands

PLATE 21.

Illustrations of the Theory of the Art of Drawing.

Figs. 1–11. Auxiliary lines
" 12–15. Proportions of the human body
" 16, 17. Proportions of the human face
" 18. Antique torso
" 19–21. Antique heads

PLATE 22.

Illustrations of the Graphic Arts.

Fig. 1. Etching on soft ground
" 2. Etching
" 3. Etching finished with the graver
" 4. Mezzotinto
" 5. Aquatint engraving
" 6. Stippling combined with line engraving

Figs. 7, 8. Manner of holding the graver
" 7a. Engraver's easel
" 8a. Engraver's hand-vice
" 9. Manipulation of cutting stones
" 9a. Engraver's oil-rubber
" 10, 11. Tampons, or dabbers
" 12. Common ruler
" 13. Parallel ruler
" 14, 15. Scrapers
" 16. Burnisher
" 17. Rocking-tool or cradle
" 18. Roulette
" 19. Scratcher
" 20–22. Etching needles
" 23–26. Gravers
" 27. Callipers
" 28ab. Improved callipers
" 29, 30. Punches,
" 31, 32. Engraver's anvil and hammer
" 33. Lines made by the cradle
" 34. Reducing frame
" 35. Frame for correctly observing curves on busts, &c.
" 36–38. Hands for engraving stamps

PLATE 23.

Alphabets of various languages for the use of engravers
⁎ The values of the letters in English characters are placed opposite them. It will suffice here to give the list of the languages whose superscriptions are in German. The only words that may require explanation are: Kehlhauch, guttural aspiration; Kurz, short; Lang, long; Werth, value; Zahlwerth, numerical value; and Benennung, name.
The alphabets are: 1. Japanese; 2. Tamul, 3. Bugic (Malay); 4. Persian arrow-headed characters; 5. Hebrew; 6. Samaritan; 7. Pehlvi (Parthian); 8. Armenian; 9. Ancient Greek; 10. Modern Greek; 11. Coptic; 12. Gothic; 13. Etruscan; 14. Anglo-Saxon; 15. Runic.

PLATE 24.

Alphabets for engravers (continued): 1. Magadha (older Sanscrit); 2. Sanscrit; 3. Tibetan; 4. Arabic; 5. Ethiopian; 6. Syriac; 7. Zend; 8. Mongolian; 9. Russian; 10. Wallachian; 11. Serbian.

GLOSSARY.

Bemerkungen, Observations; these are: * Jerr adds to the force of the preceding consonant; ** Jehr softens the preceding consonant; *** The Serbian language is printed with Russian type, with the addition of Jerr and Jehr.
Interpuctionszeichen der Zendschrift, Punctuation marks of the Zend language.

PLATE 25.

Figs. 1–33. Details illustrating the construction of theatrical buildings

PLATE 26.

Figs. 1–45. Details illustrating the construction of theatrical buildings

Architecture, Plate 2

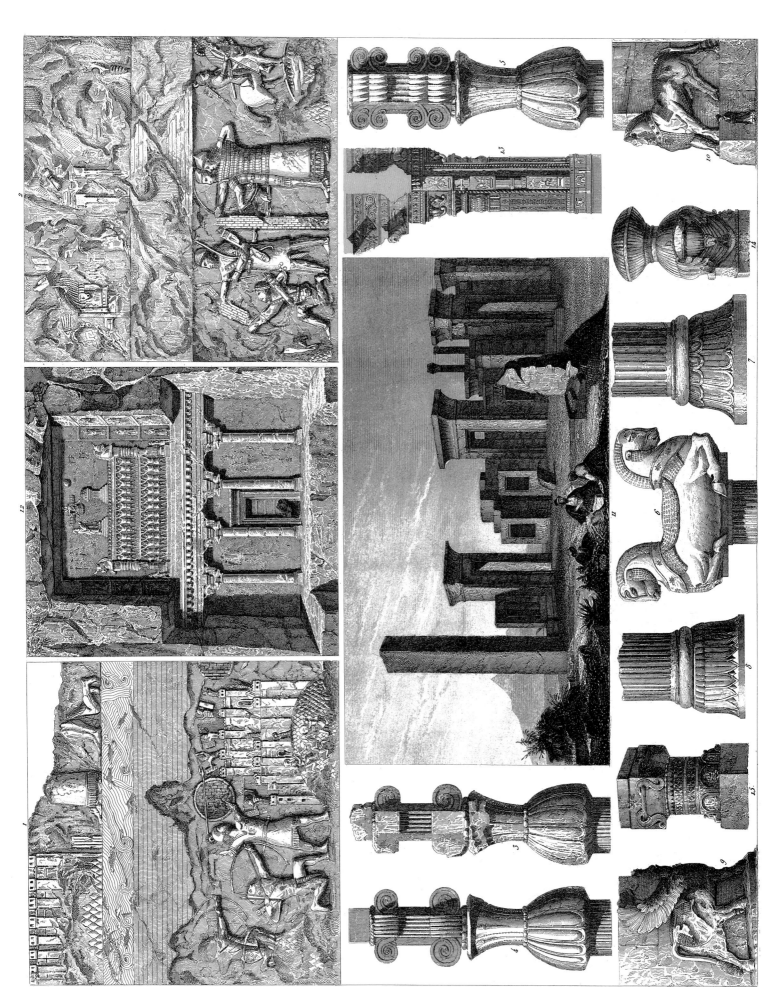

Architecture, Plate 4

4

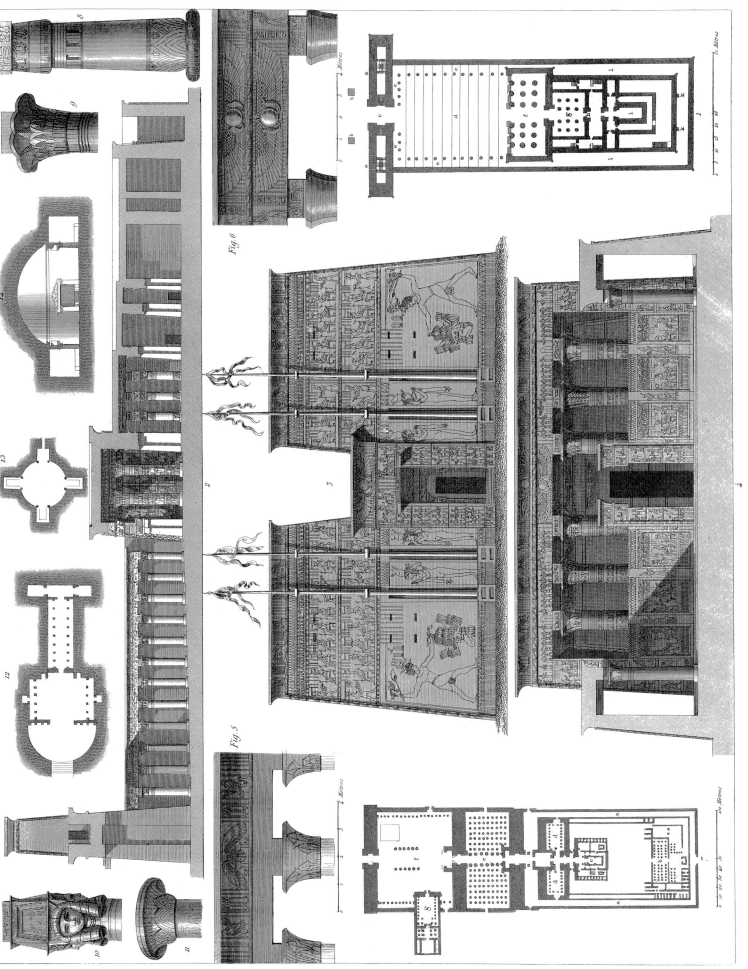
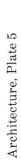

Fig. 6

Fig. 5

Fig. 3

Architecture, Plate 5

Maasstab für Figur 3 et 4.

Maasstab für Figur 2.

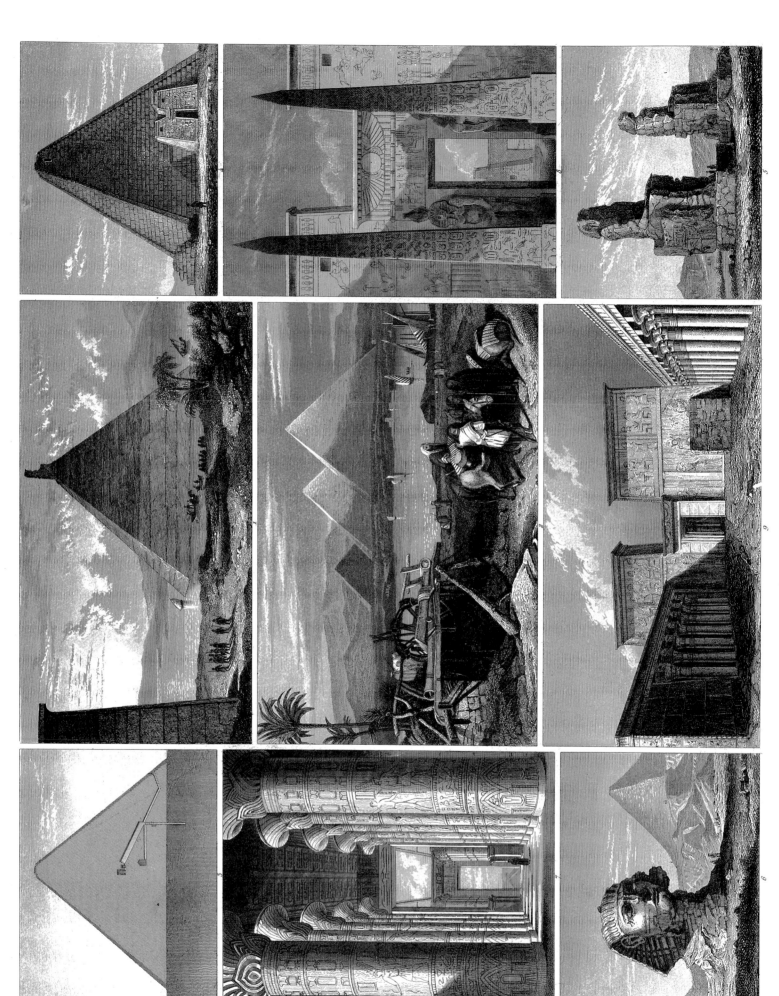

Architecture, Plate 6

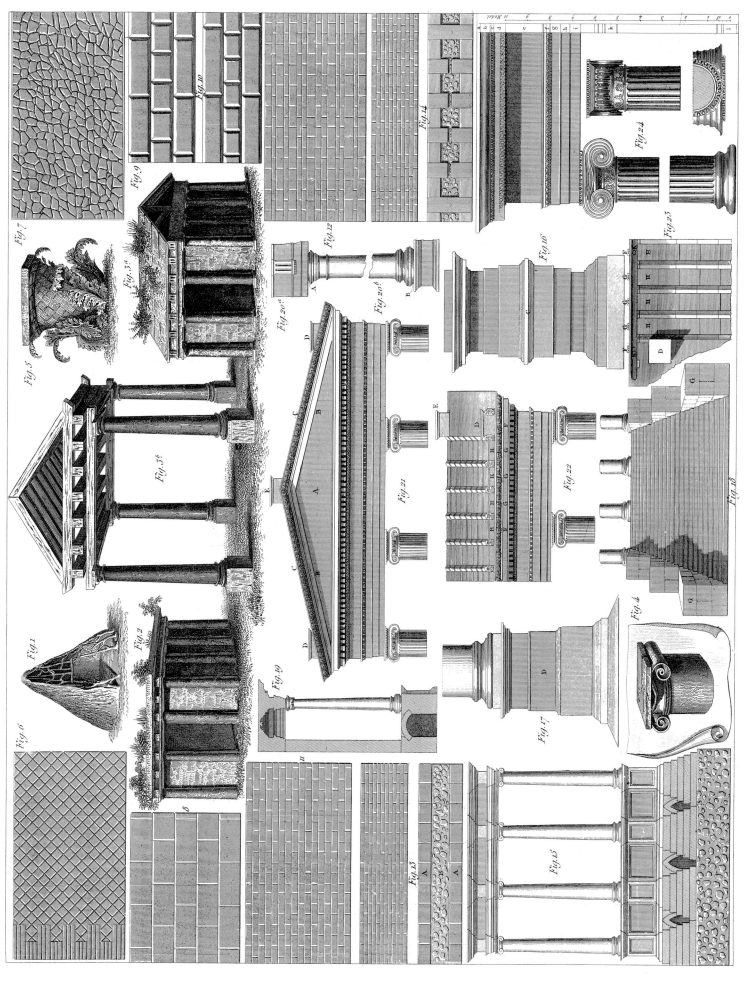

Architecture, Plate 8

Architecture, Plate 9

9

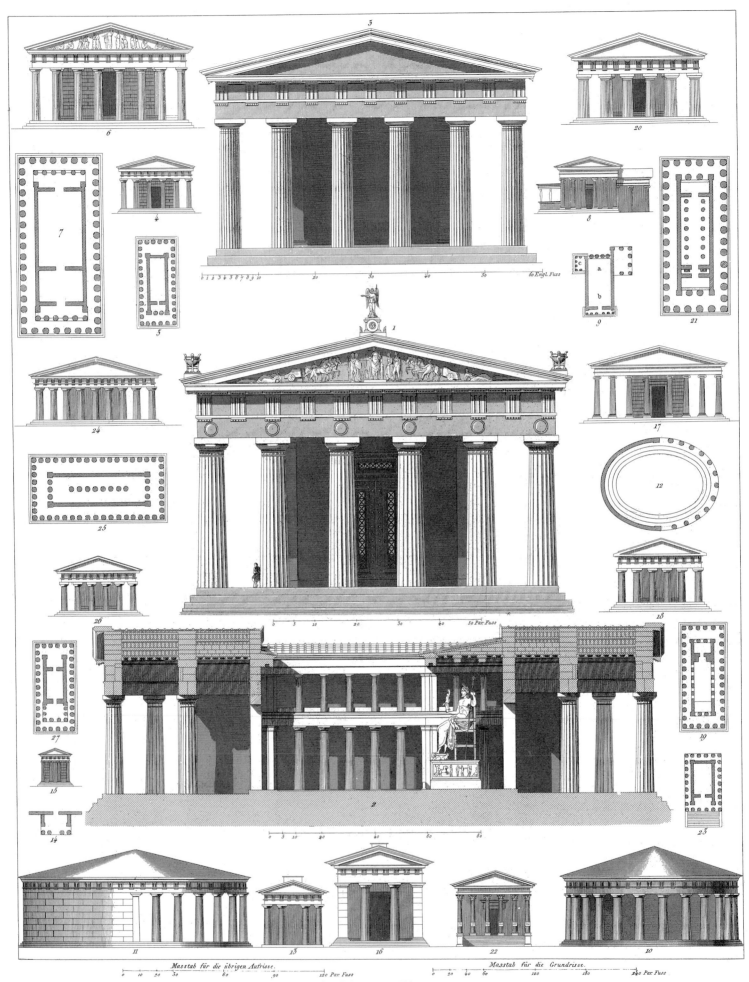

Maasstäbe für die Grundrisse Fig. 8, 19, 13....20.
3m Griech. Fuss.

Architecture, Plate 11

11

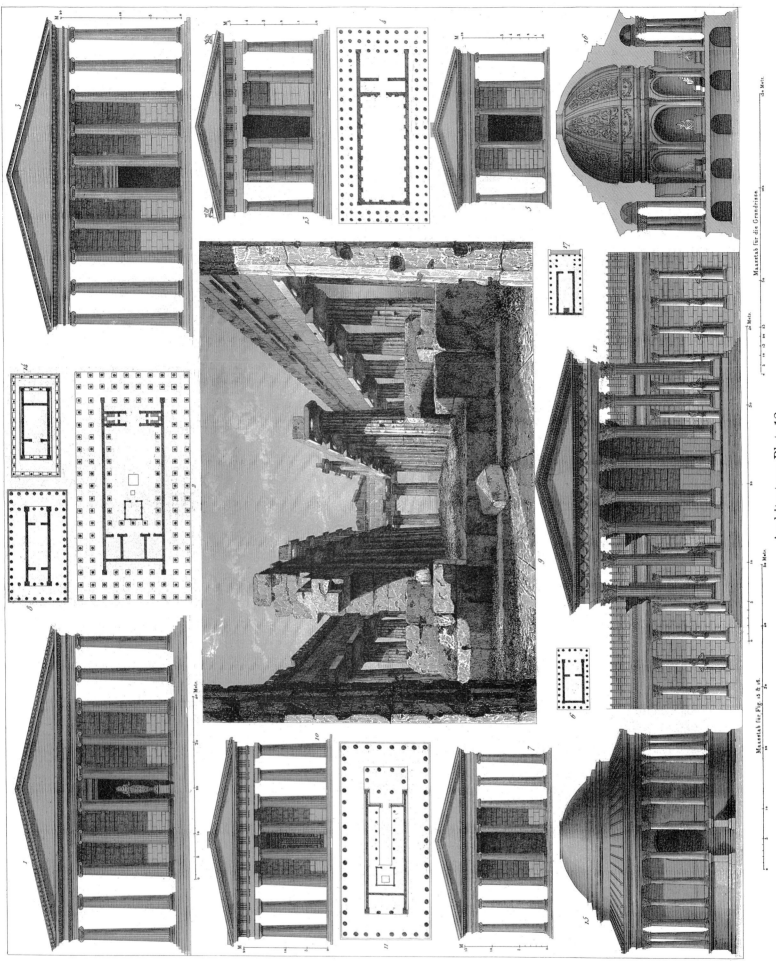

Architecture, Plate 12

Architecture, Plate 13

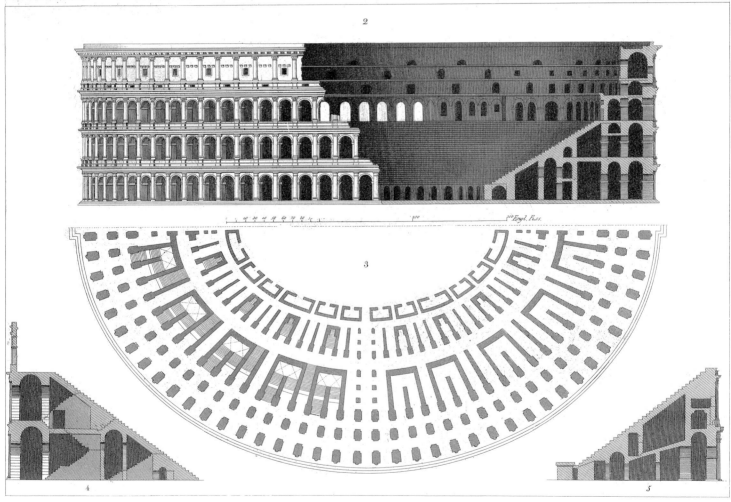

Architecture, Plate 14

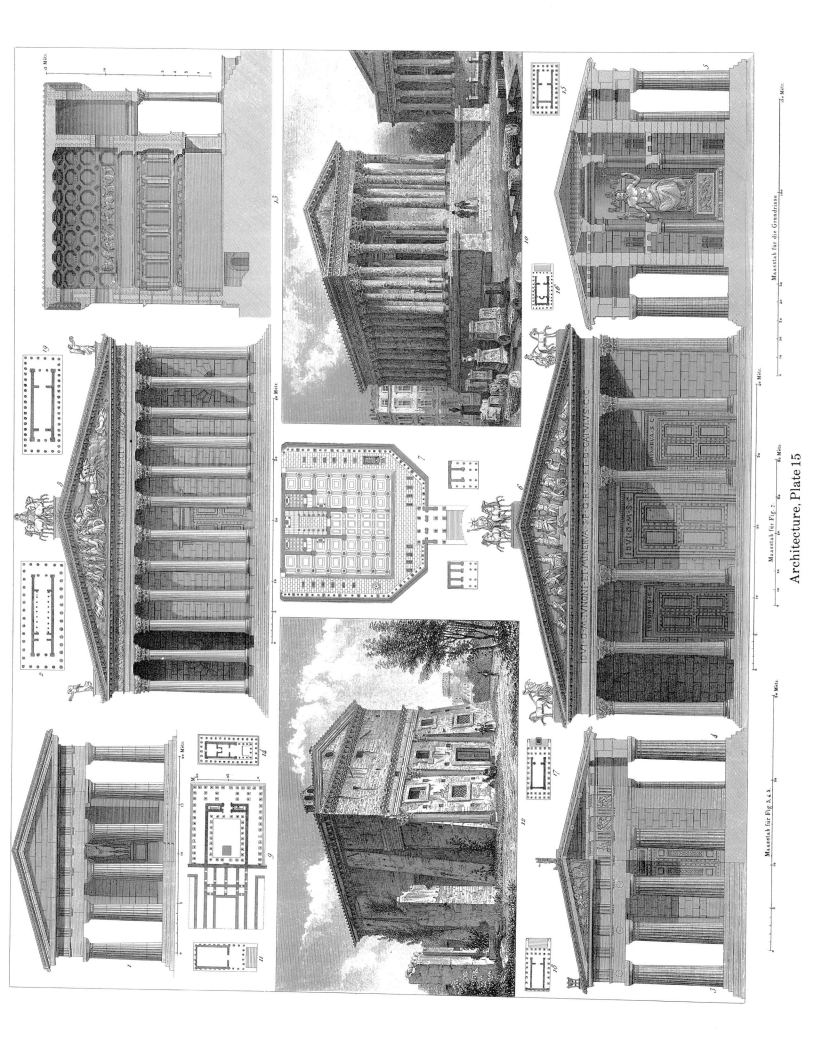

Architecture, Plate 15

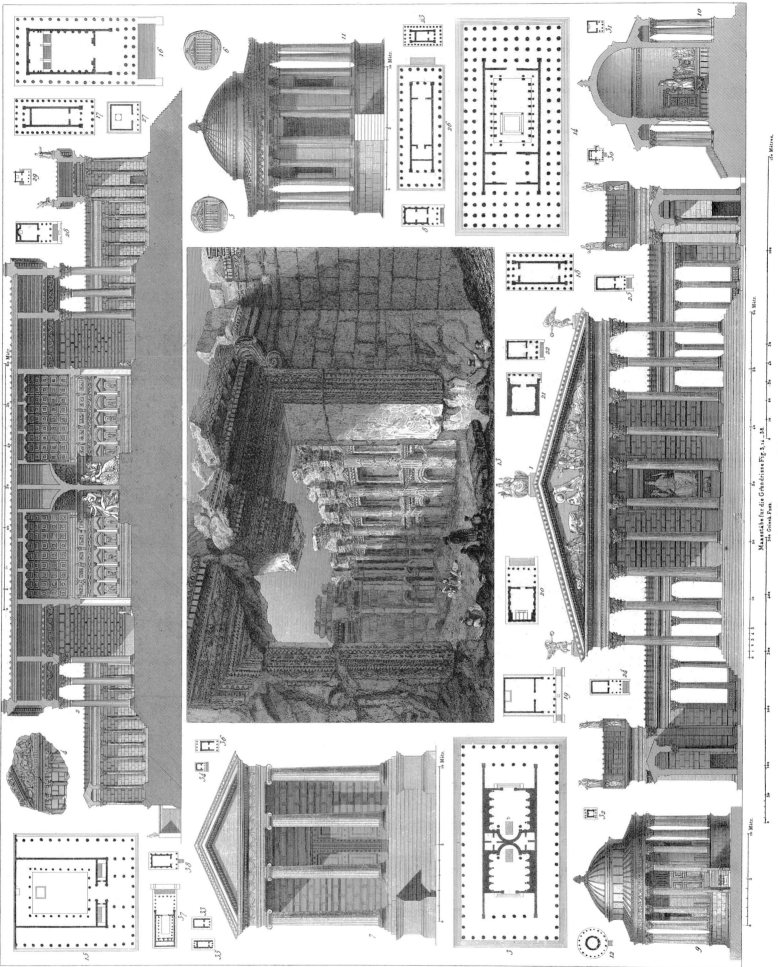

Architecture, Plate 16

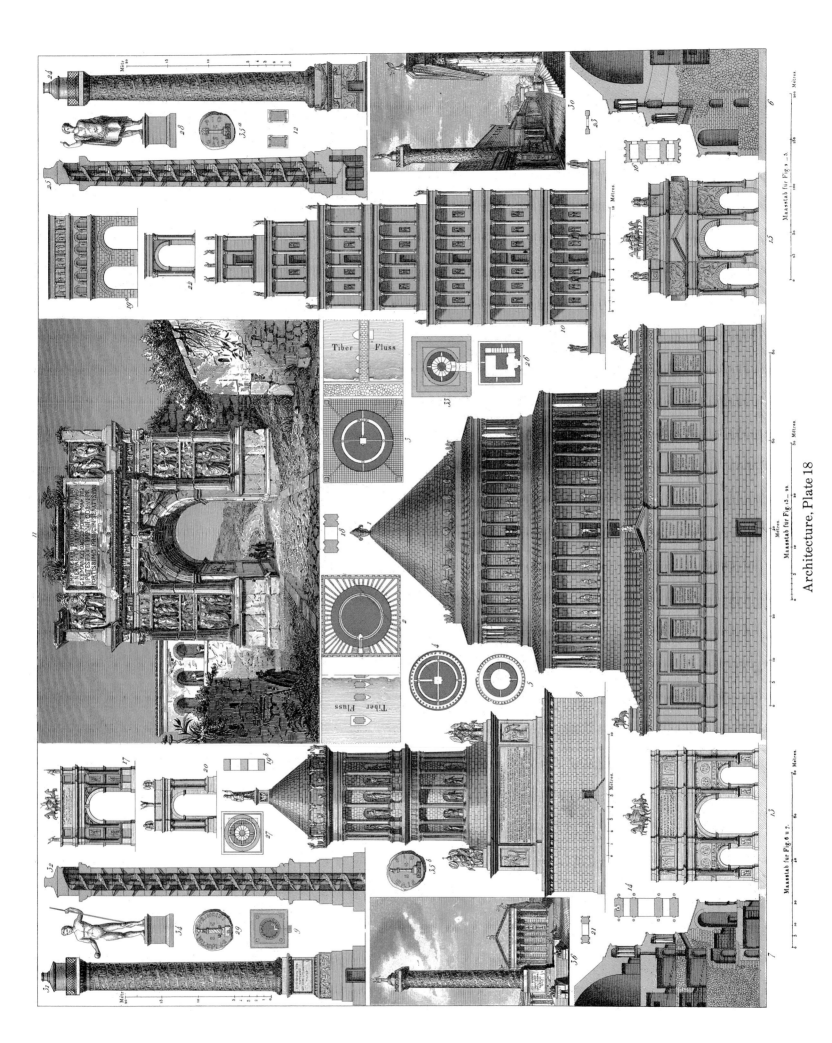

Architecture, Plate 18

Tiber Fluss

Tiber Fluss

Maasstab für Fig. 13—23.

Maasstab für Fig. 2—5.

Maasstab für Fig. 6 u. 7.

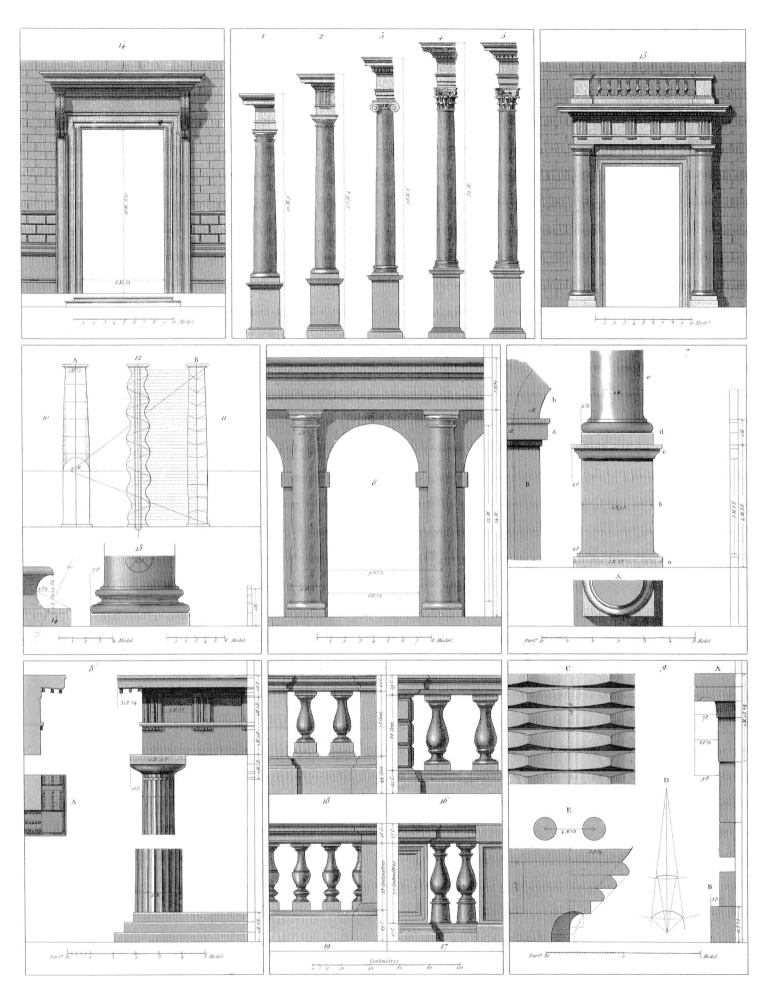

Architecture, Plate 20

Architecture, Plate 21

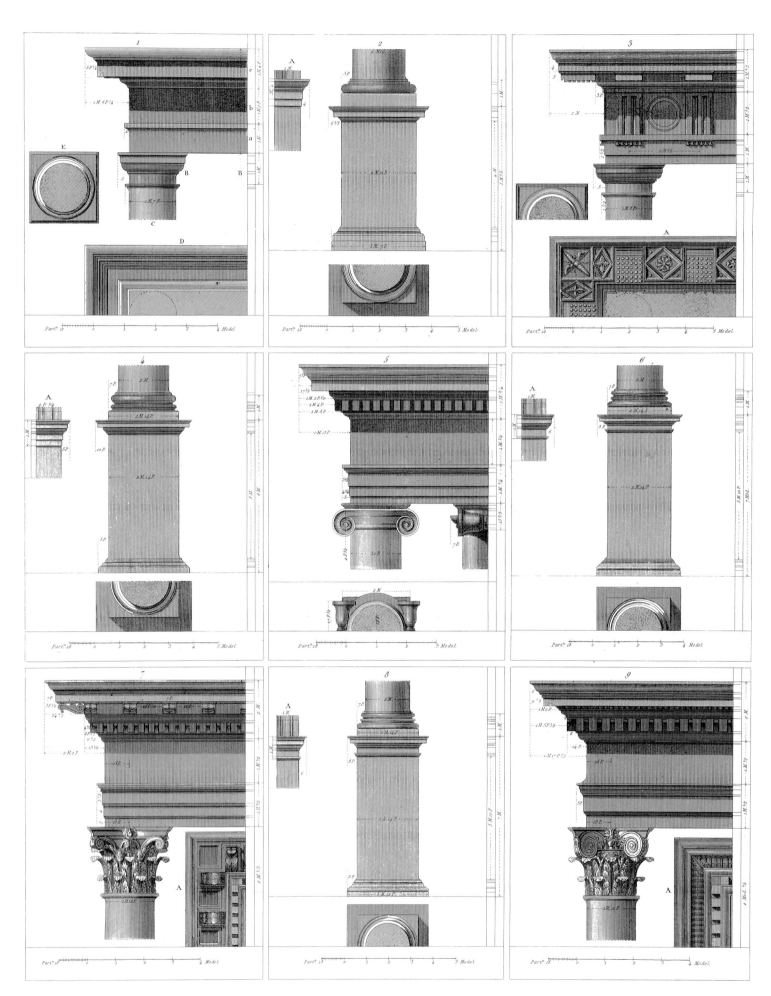

Architecture, Plate 22

Architecture, Plate 23

Architecture, Plate 25

25

Architecture, Plate 27

Architecture, Plate 28

Maasstab für Fig. 4. 16

Maasstab für Fig. 4. 16

Maasstab für Fig. 5. 6

28

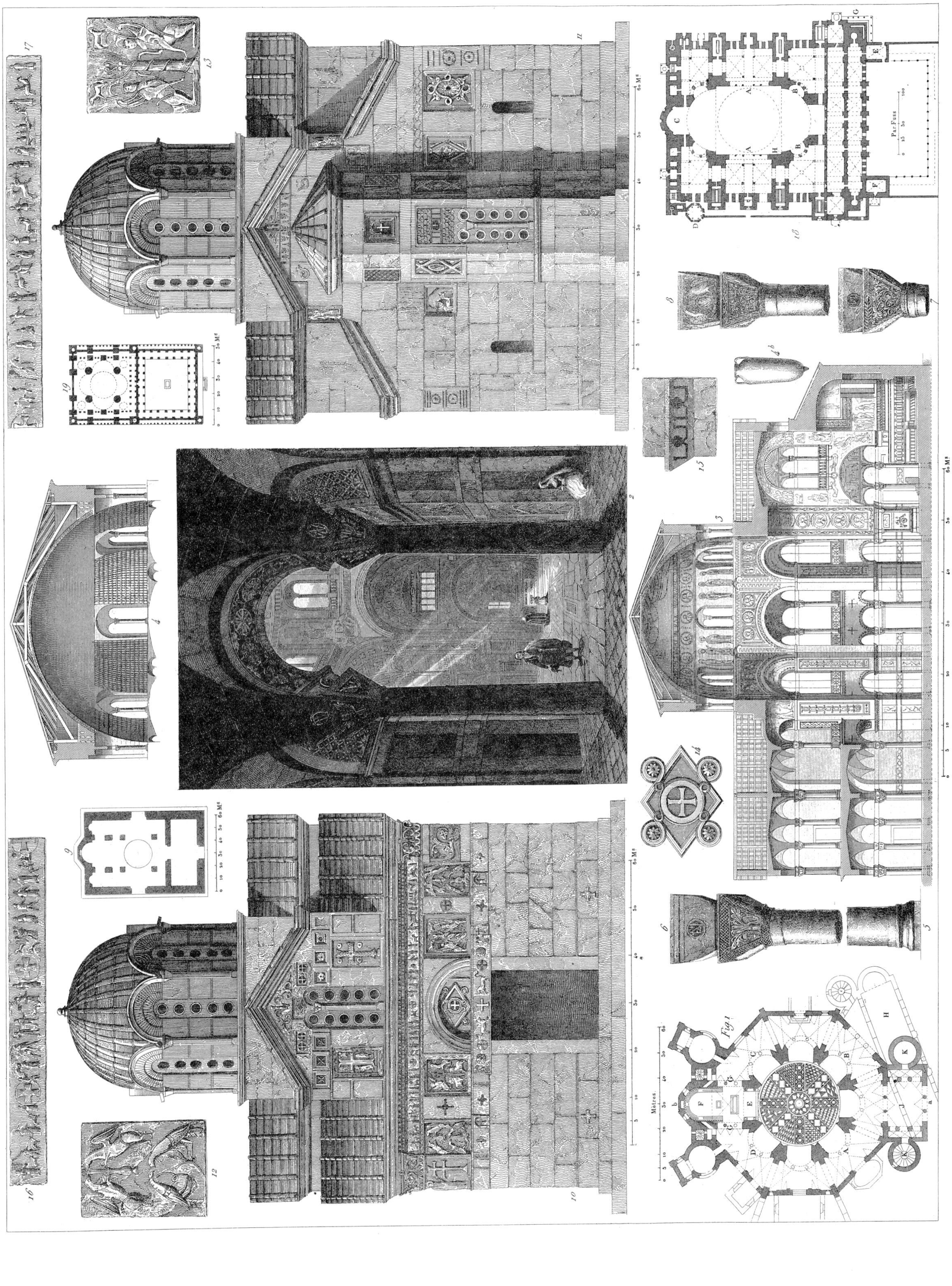

Architecture, Plate 29

29

Architecture, Plate 30

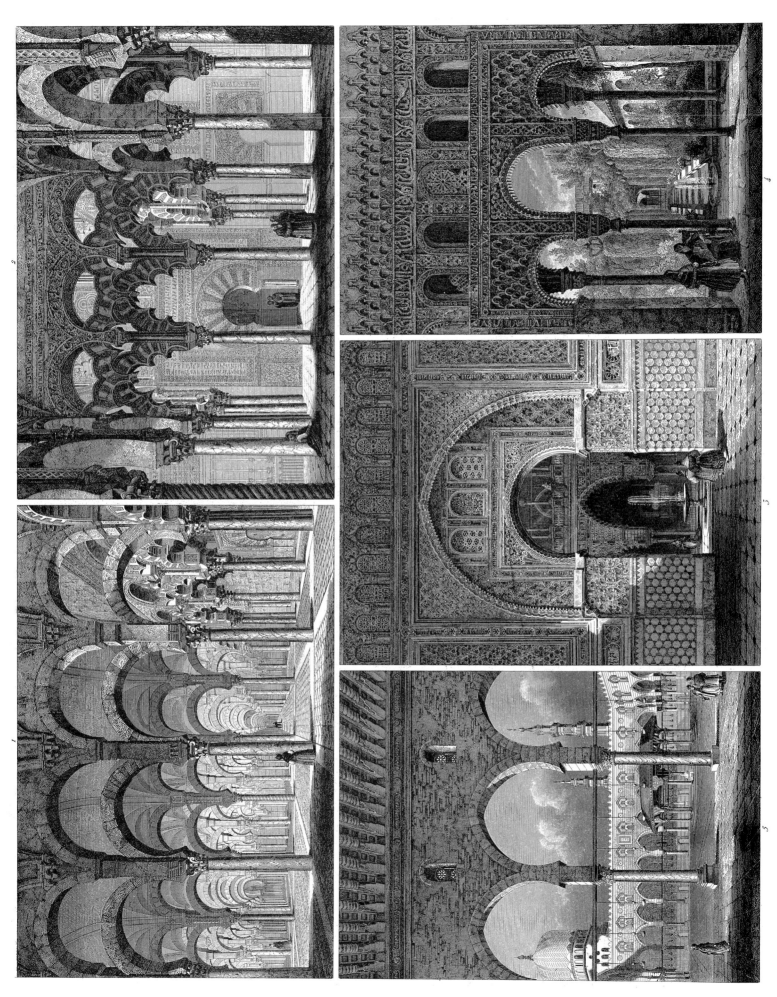

Architecture, Plate 32

Architecture, Plate 33

34

Architecture, Plate 35

Architecture, Plate 36

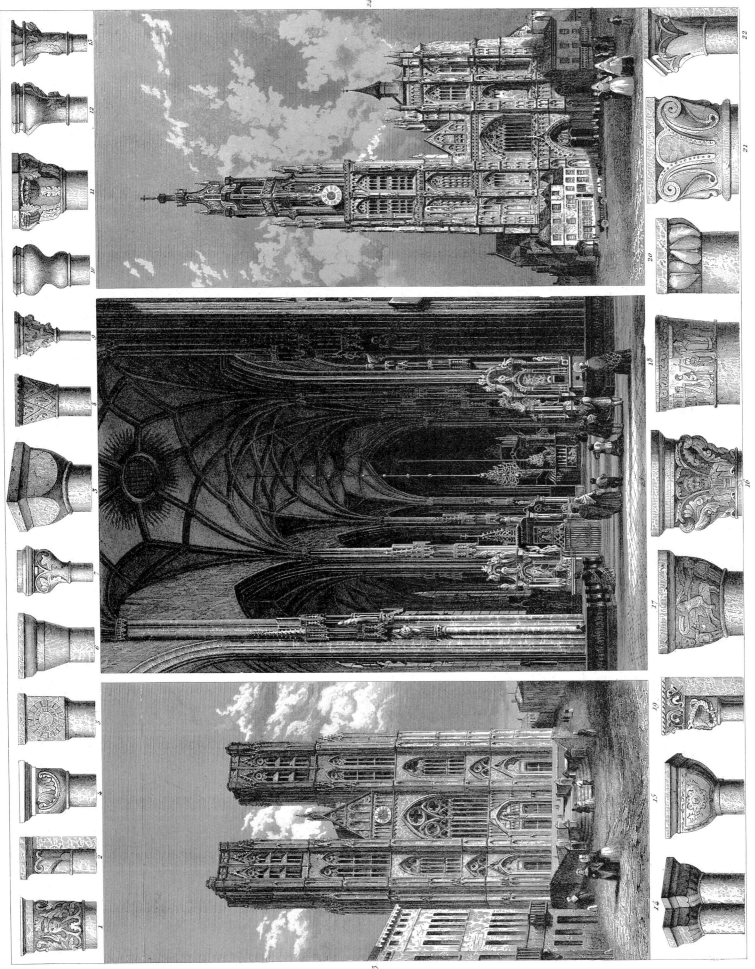

Architecture, Plate 37

37

Architecture, Plate 38

38

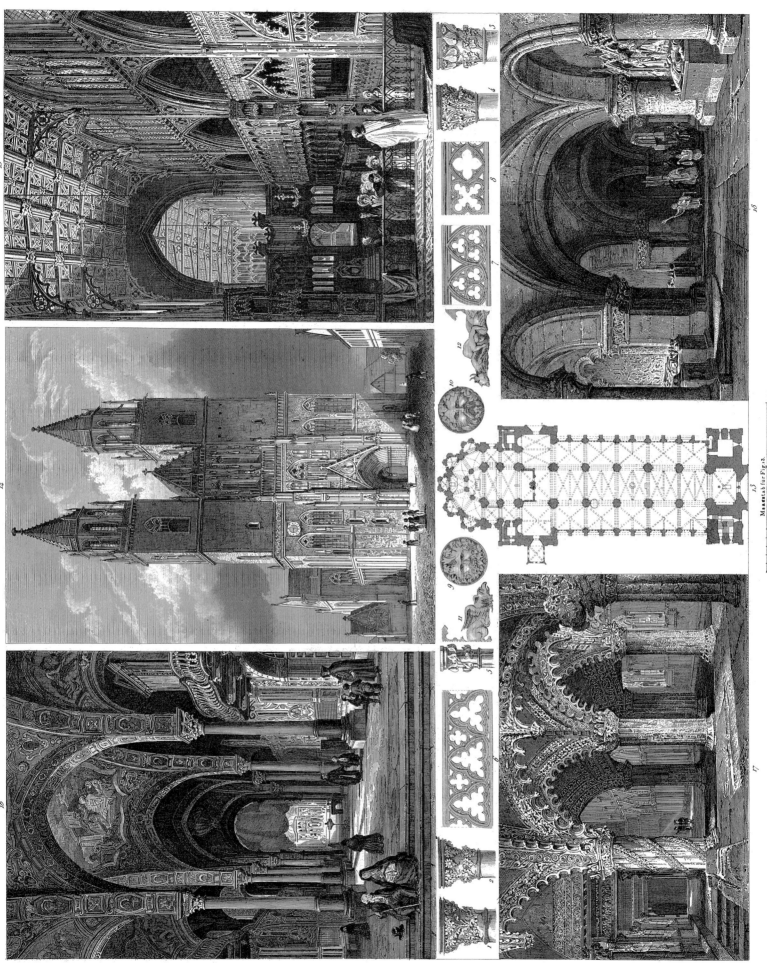

Architecture, Plate 41

Architecture, Plate 42

Architecture, Plate 43

43

Fig. 2

Fig. 1

Metres

Metres

Metres

Architecture, Plate 44

Architecture, Plate 45

45

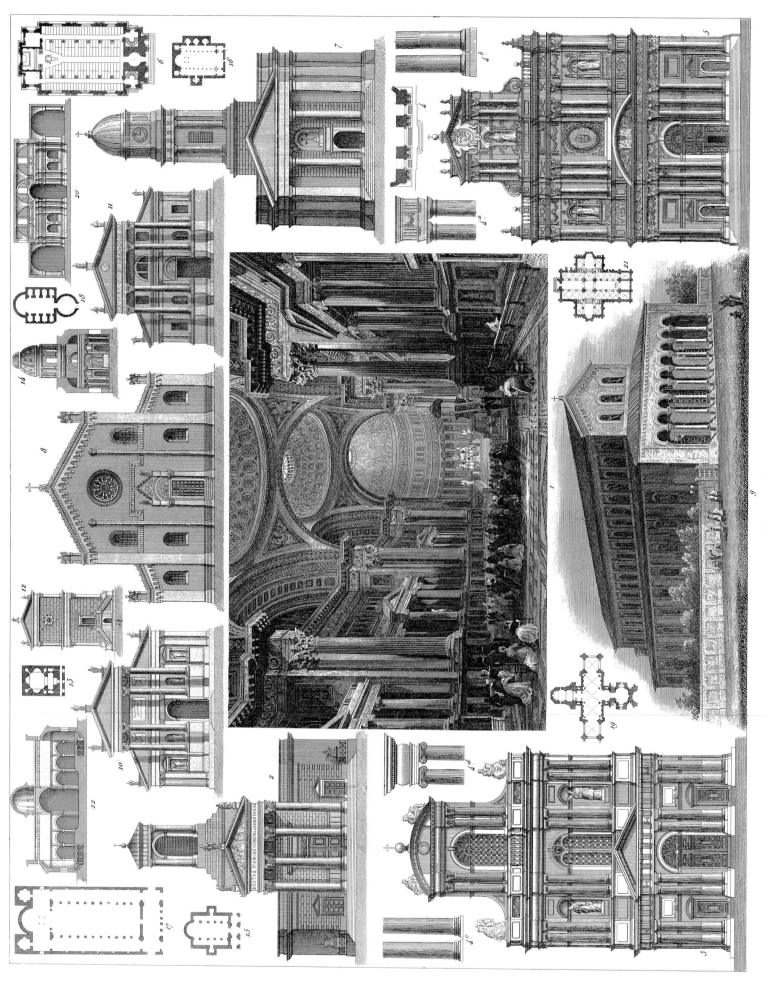

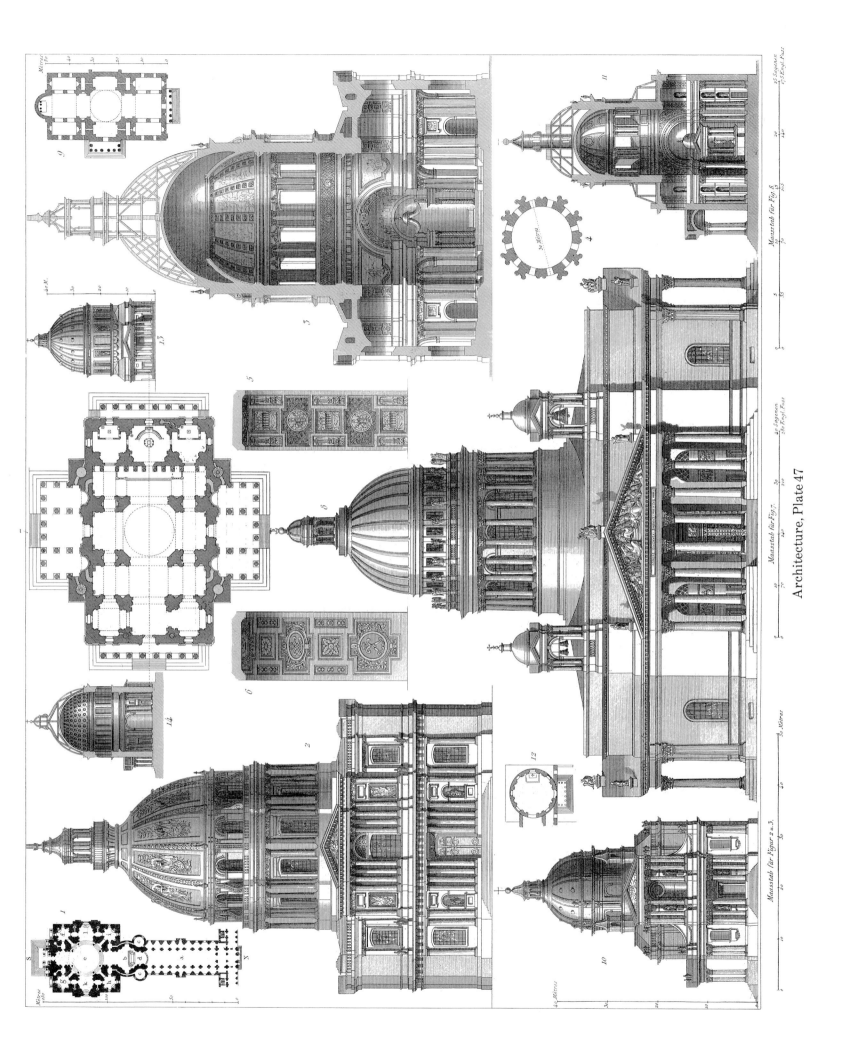

Architecture, Plate 47

47

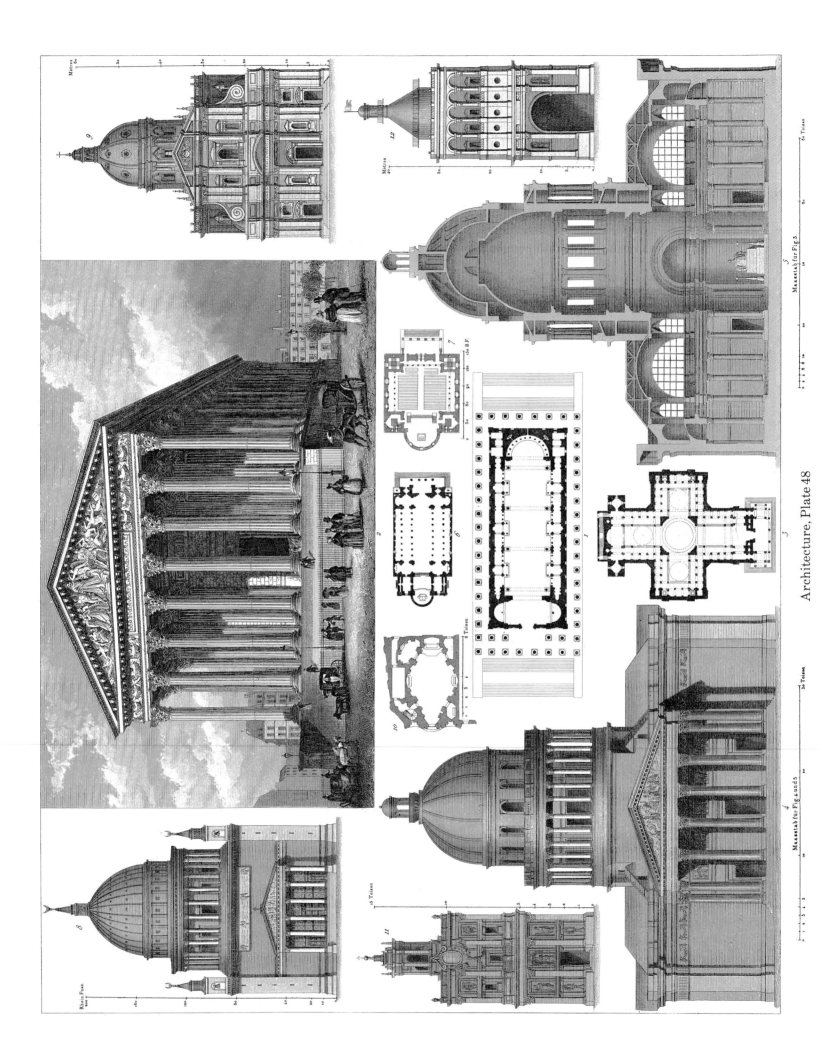

Architecture, Plate 48

48

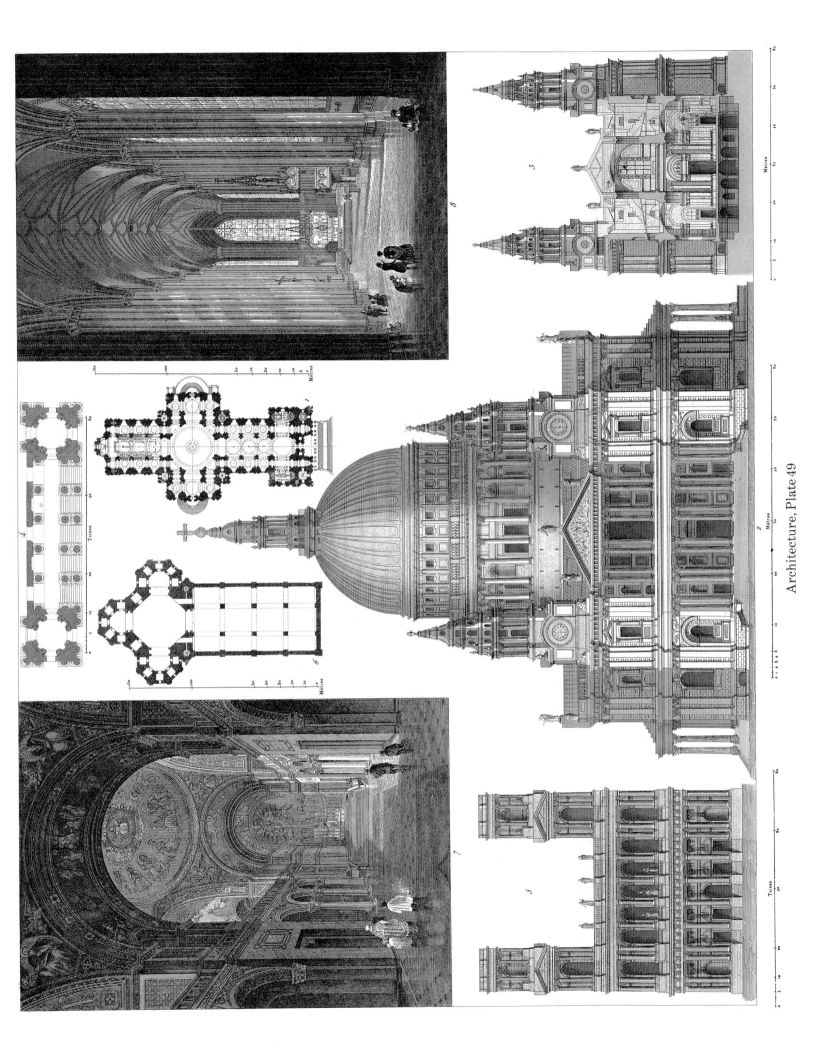

Architecture, Plate 49

Architecture, Plate 50

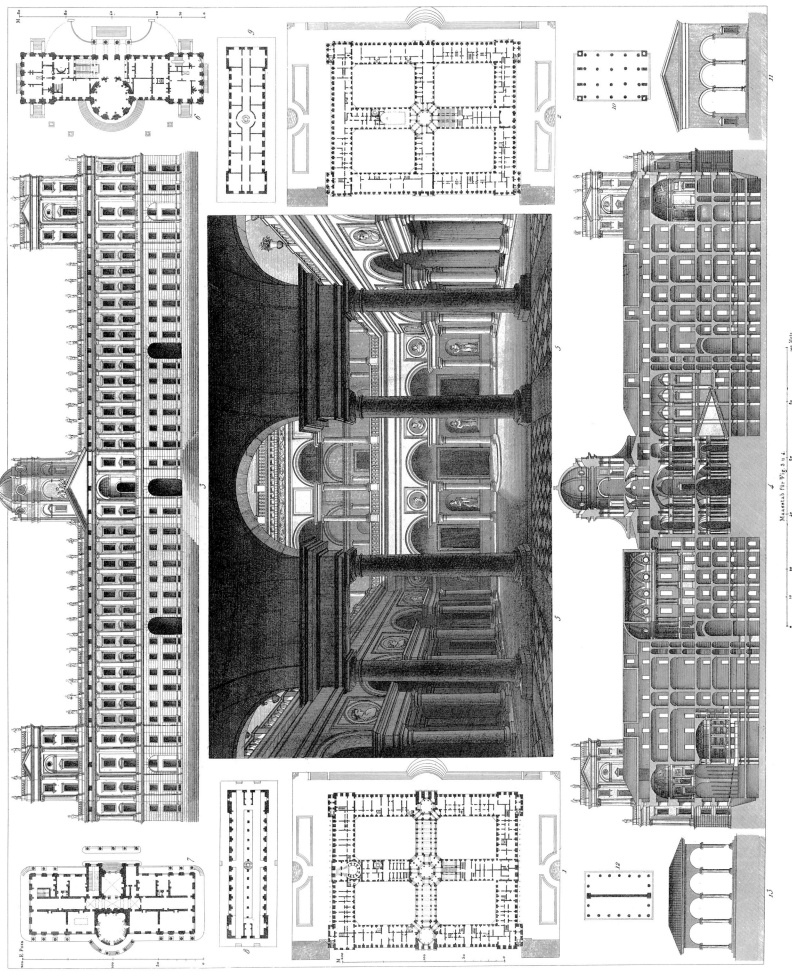

Architecture, Plate 51

Maasstab für die Figuren 8, 10ᵃ·ᵇ·ᶜ

Maasstab für die Figuren 3—9.

Architecture, Plate 52

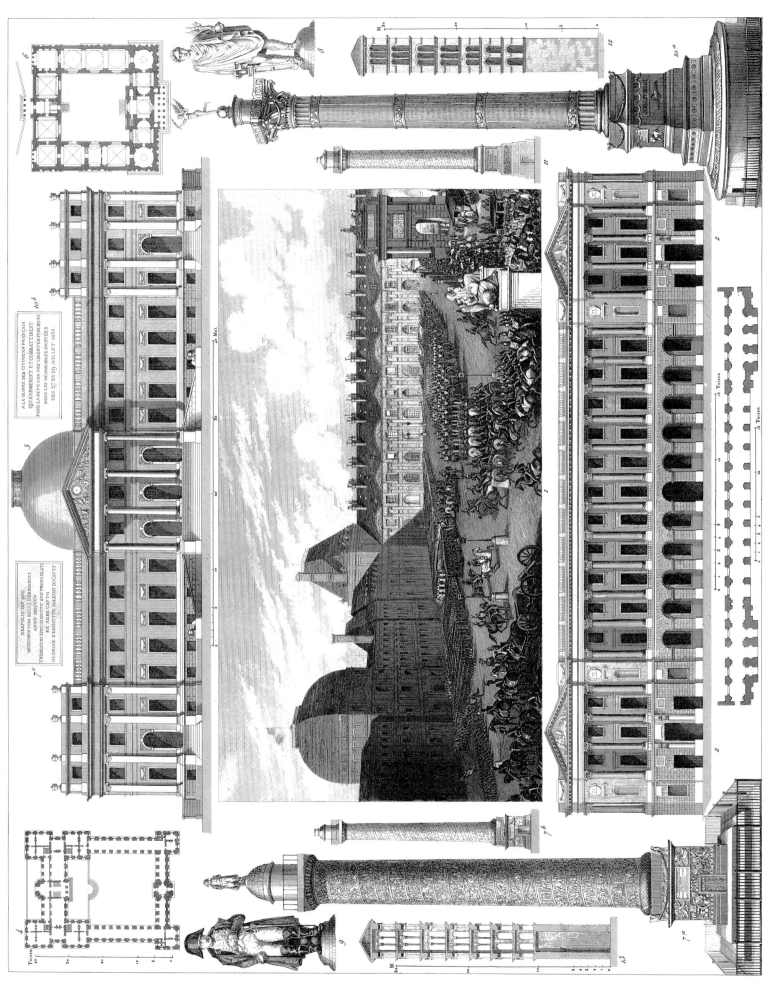

Architecture, Plate 54

54

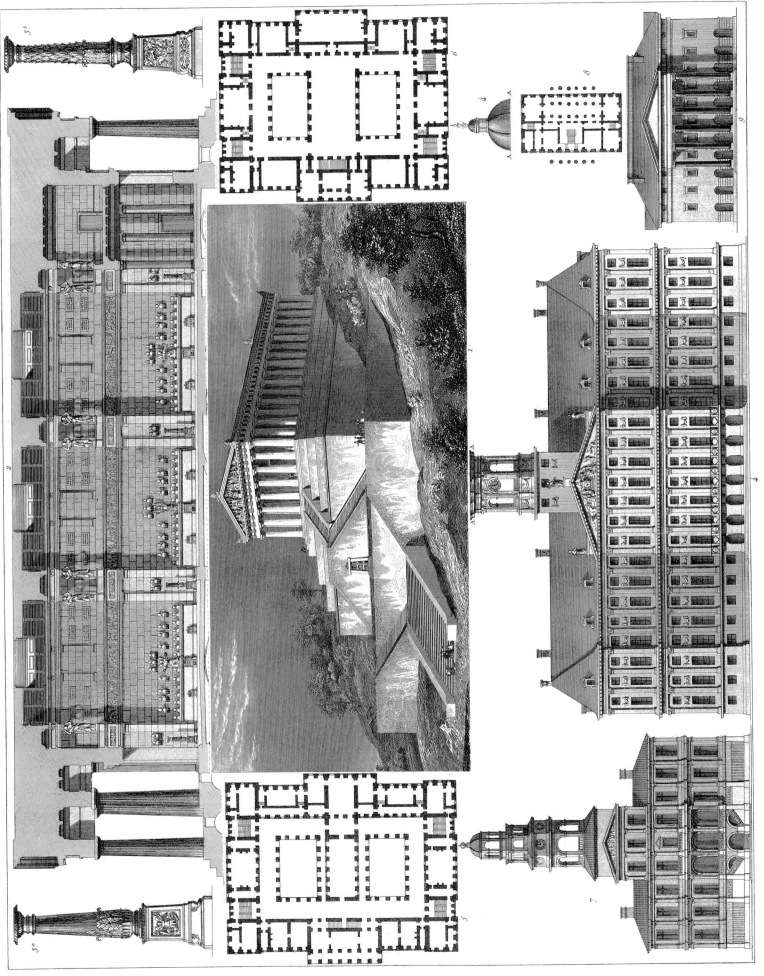

Architecture, Plate 55

55

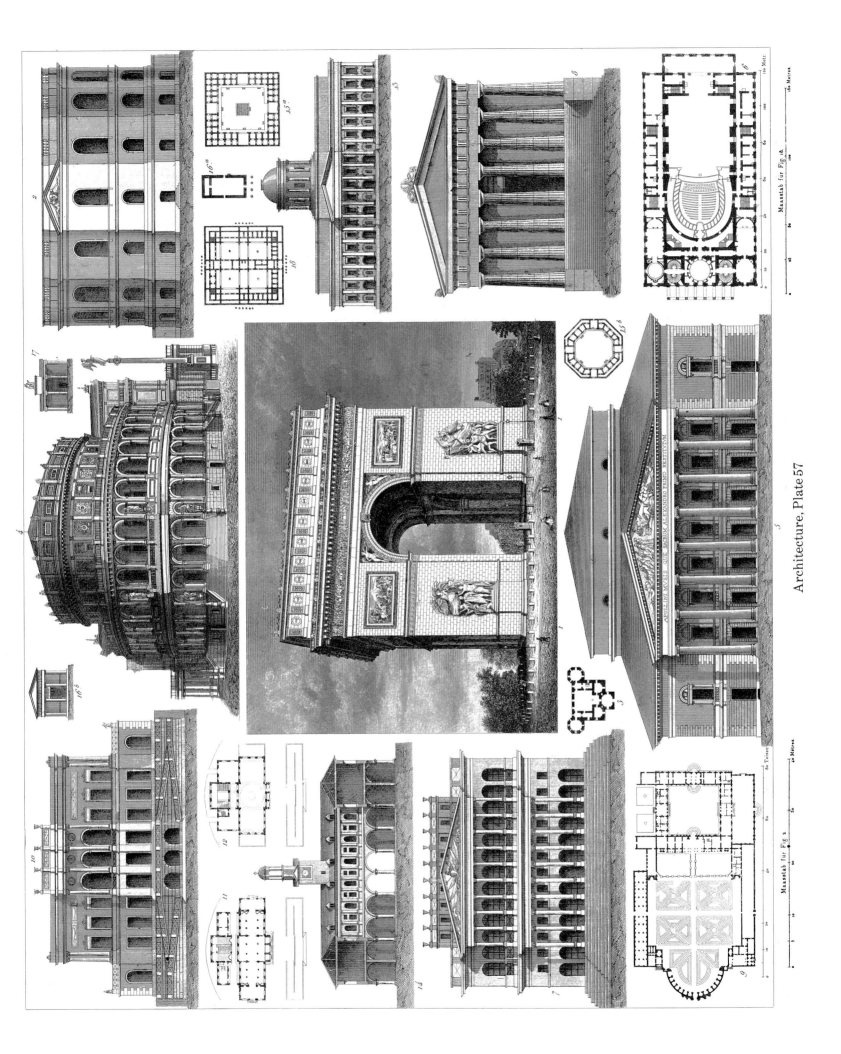

Architecture, Plate 57

APOLLINI MVSIS QVE SACRVM ALEXANDRO PRIMO RESTIVVM

Maasstab für Fig. 18.

Maasstab für Fig. 2.

57

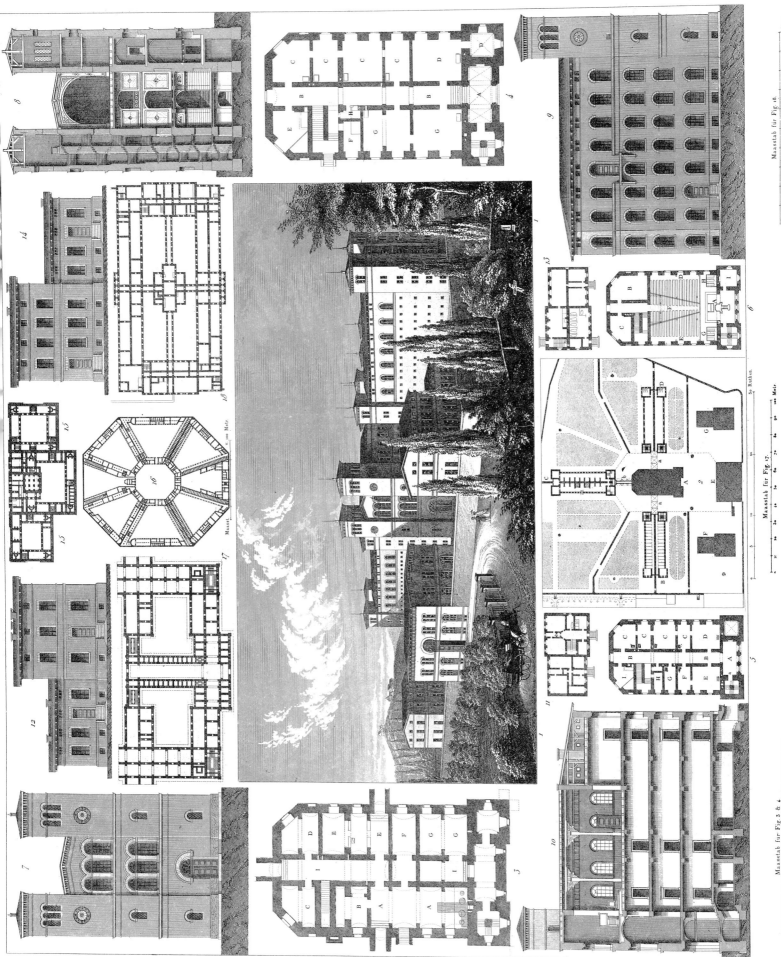

Architecture, Plate 59

Mythology, Plate 1

61

Mythology, Plate 2

62

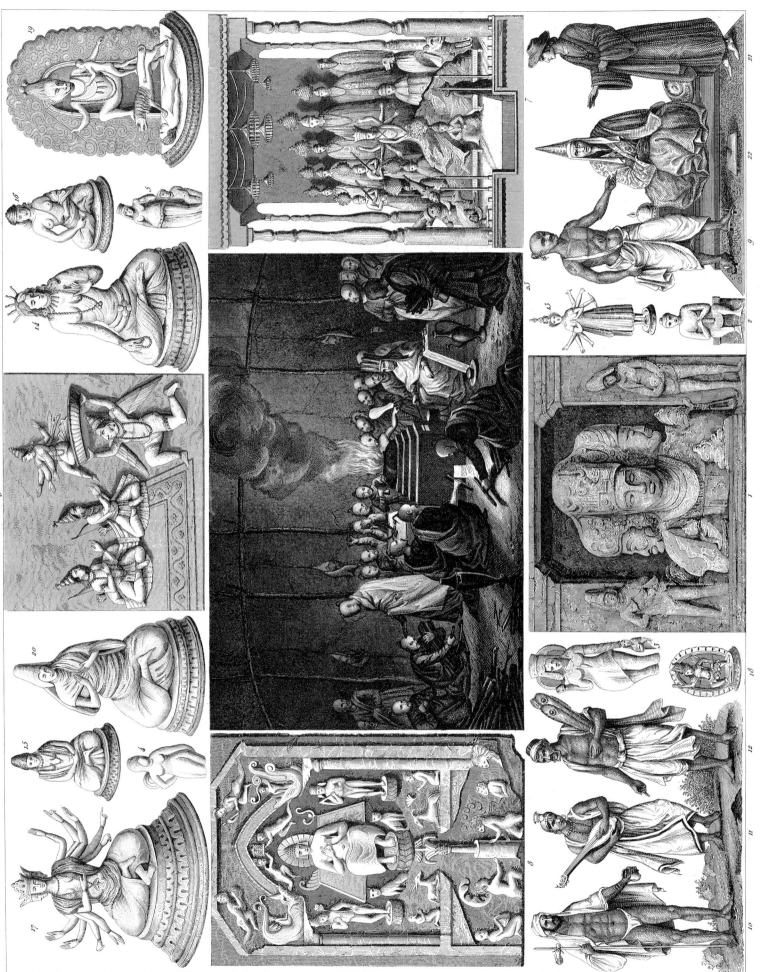

Mythology, Plate 3

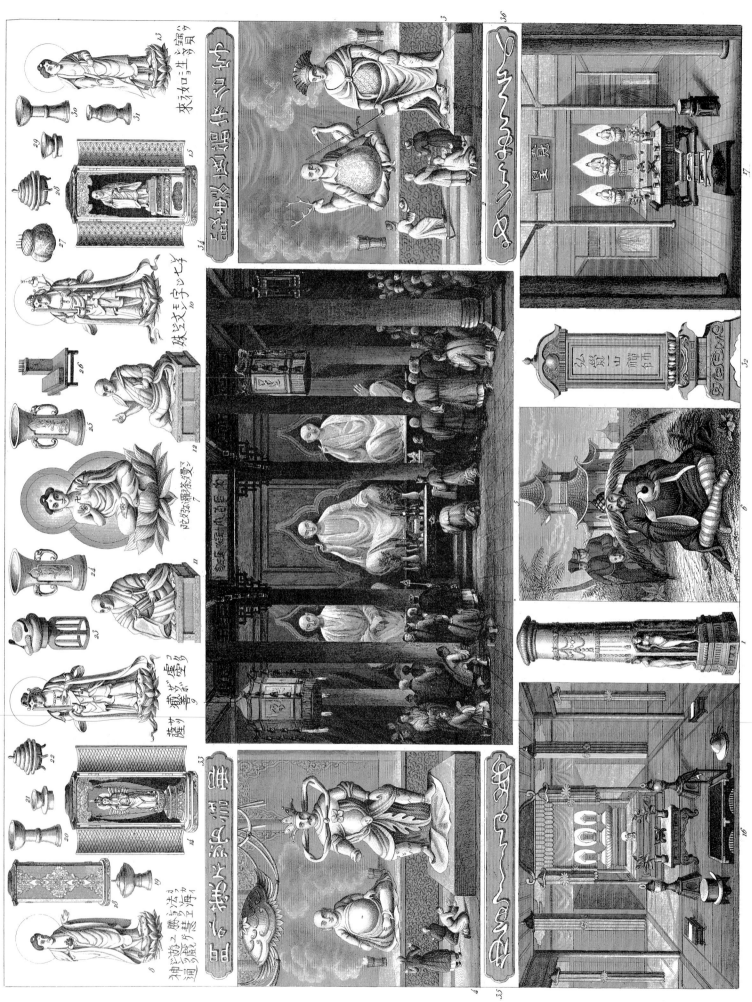

Mythology, Plate 4

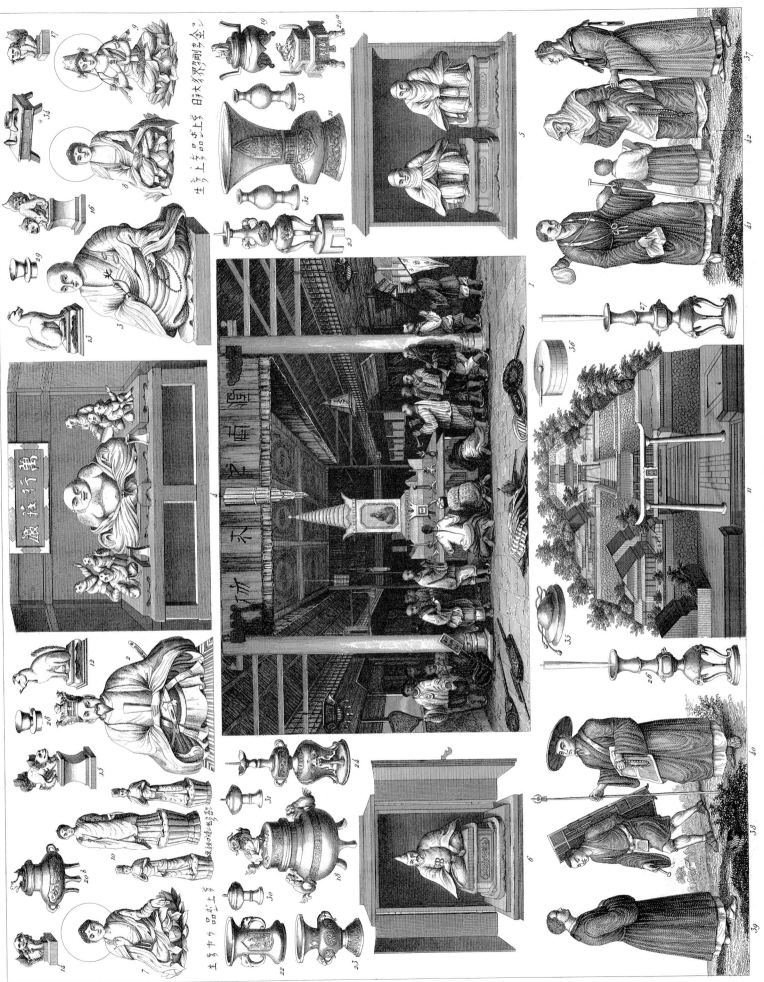

Mythology, Plate 5

65

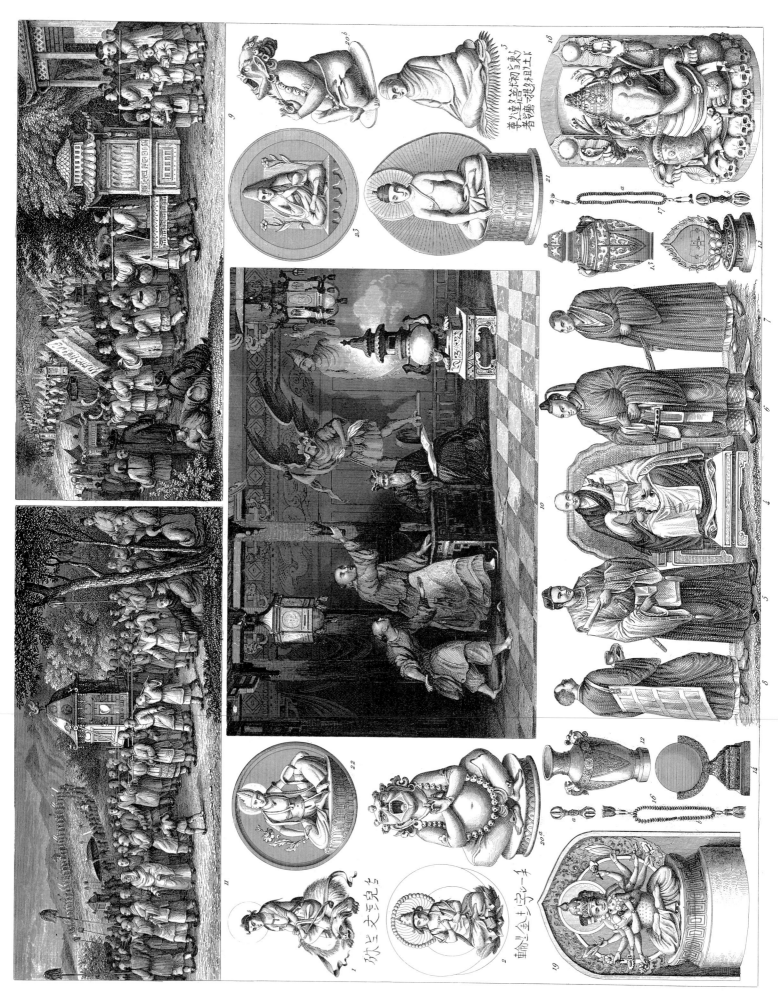

Mythology, Plate 6

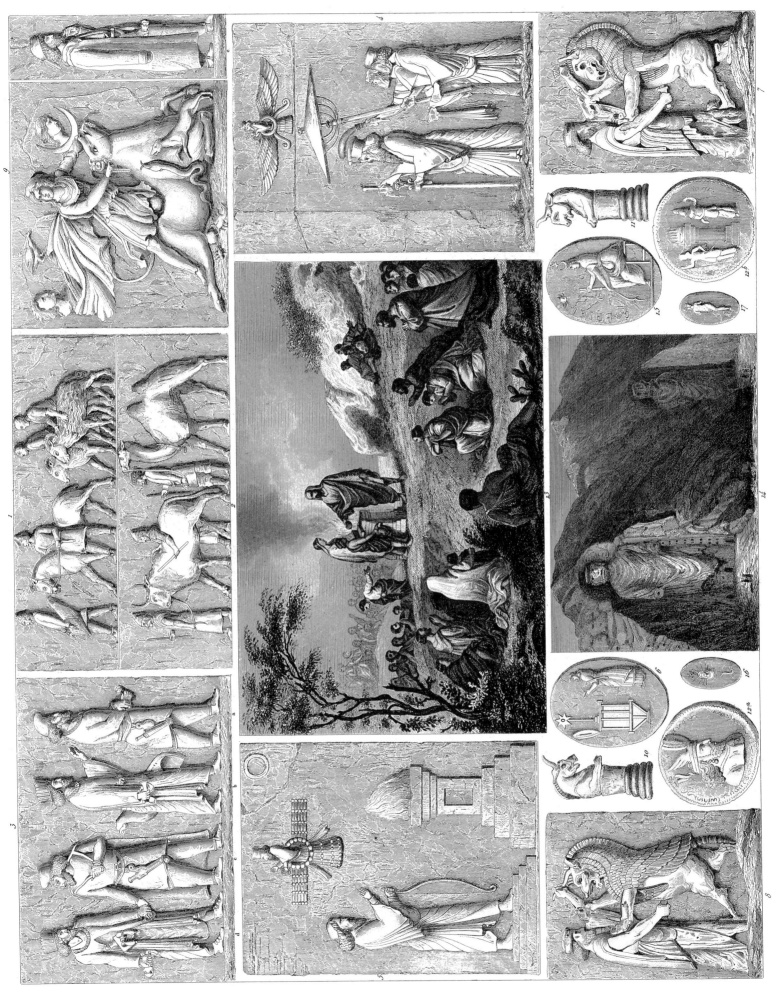

Mythology, Plate 7

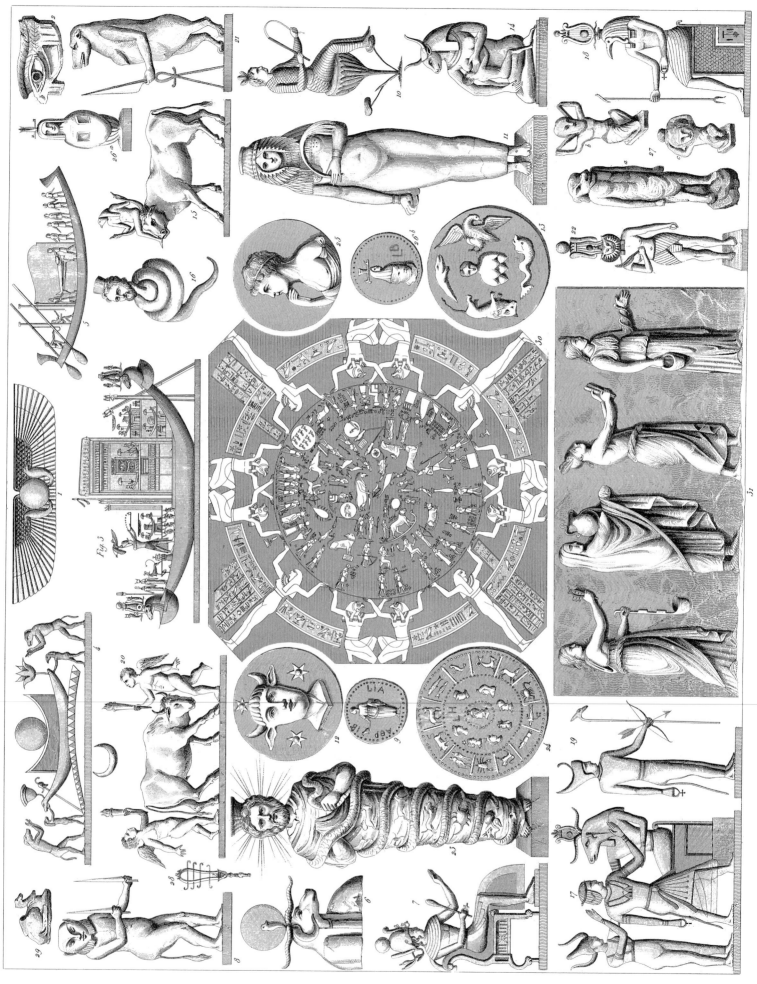

Mythology, Plate 8

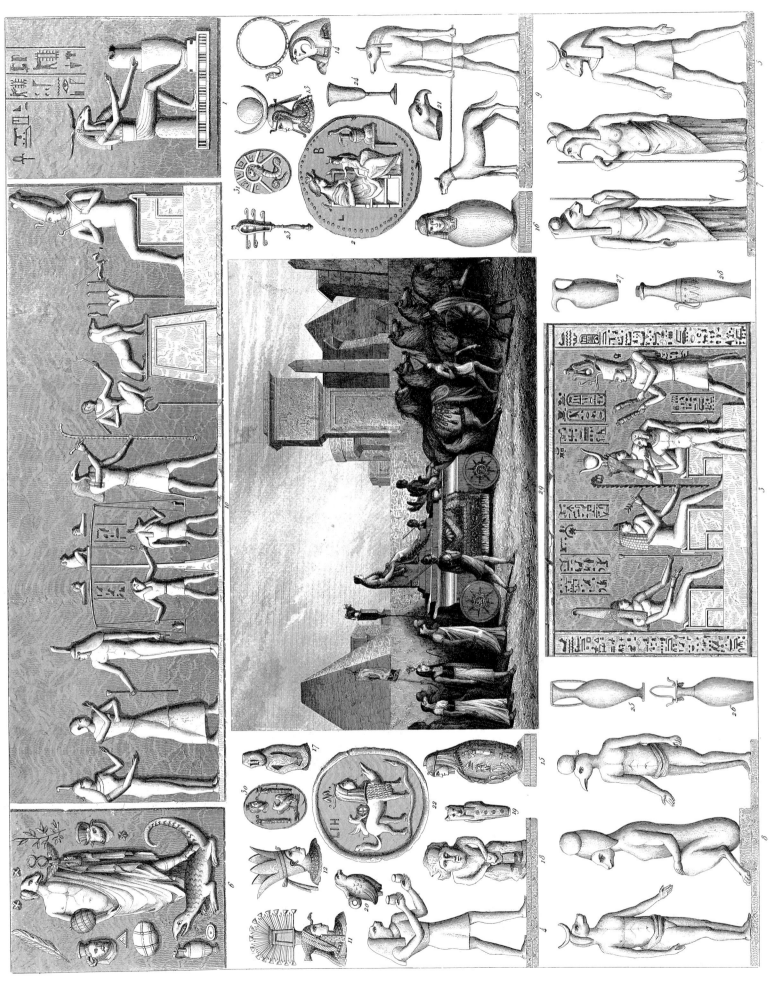

Mythology, Plate 9

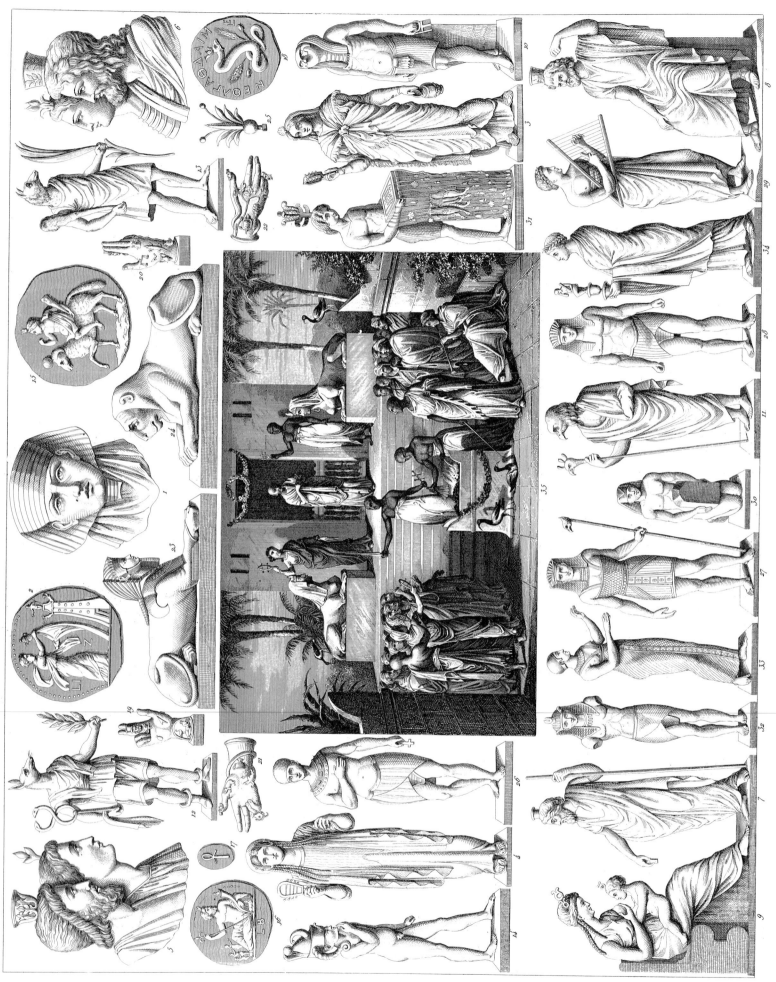

Mythology, Plate 10

Mythology, Plate 11

71

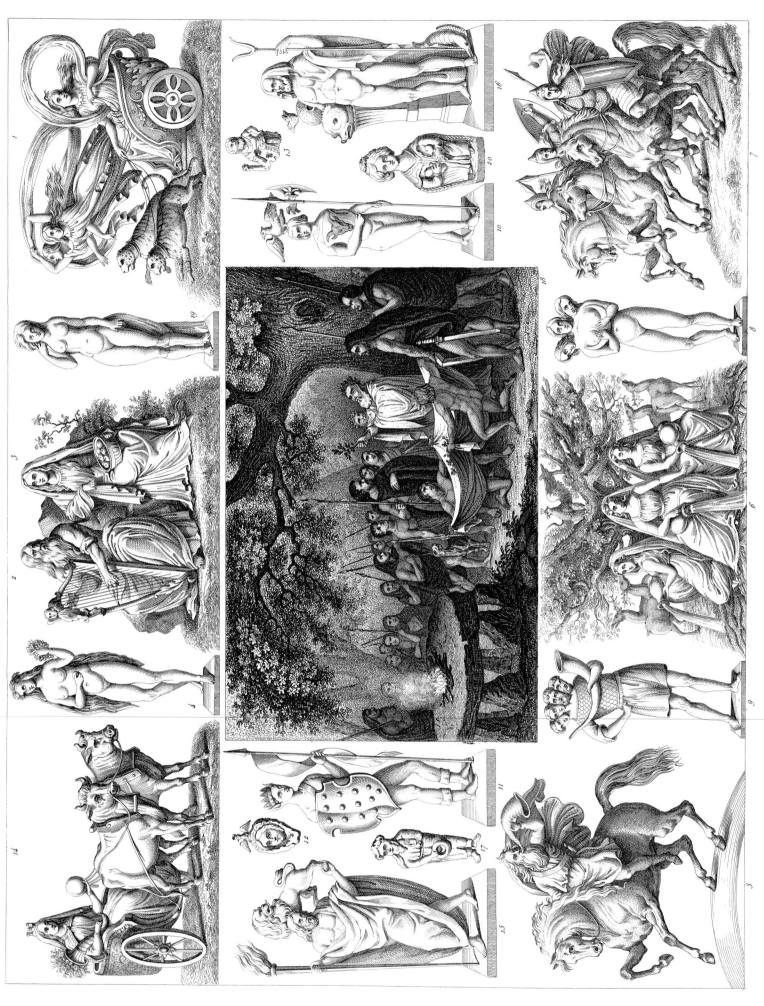

Mythology, Plate 12

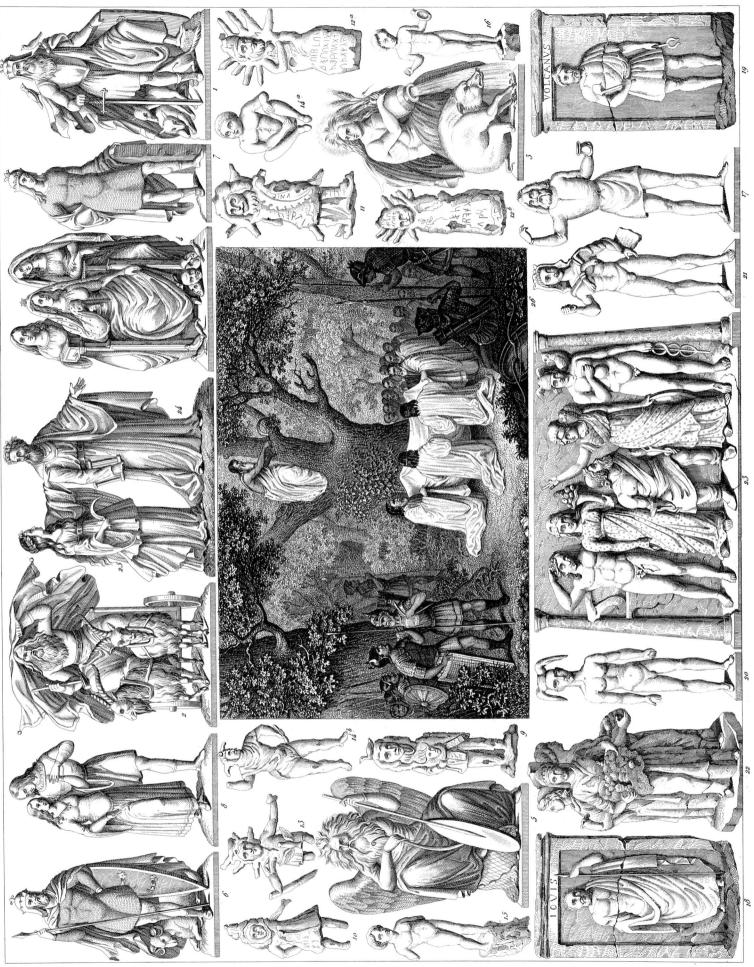

Mythology, Plate 13

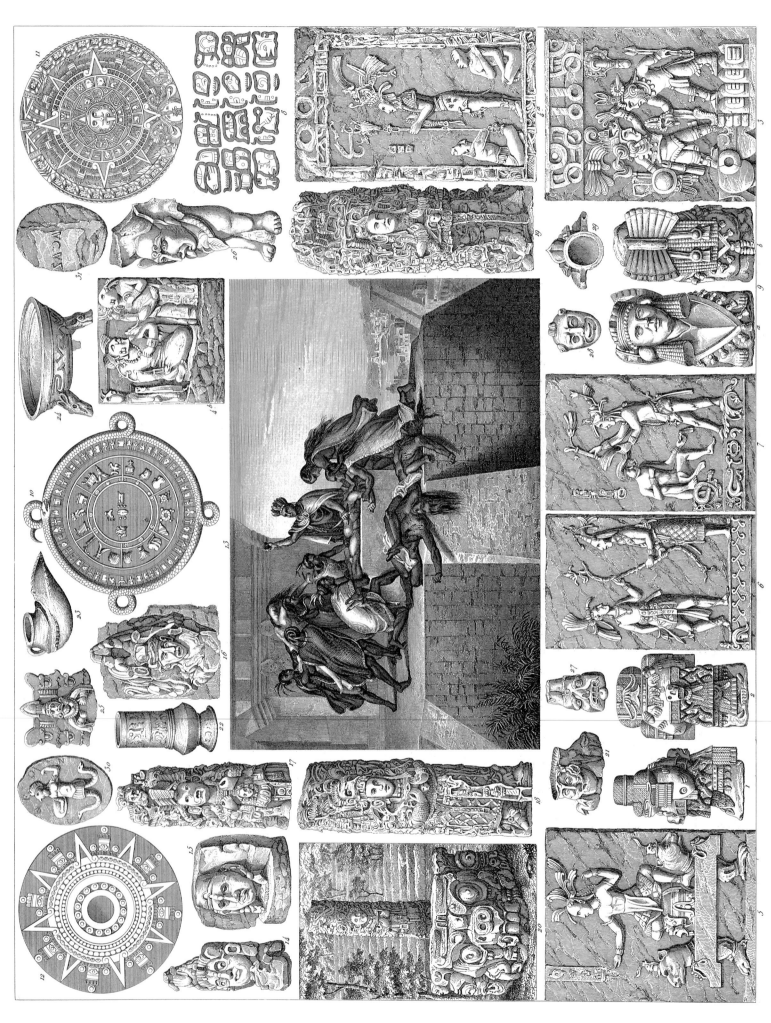

Mythology, Plate 14

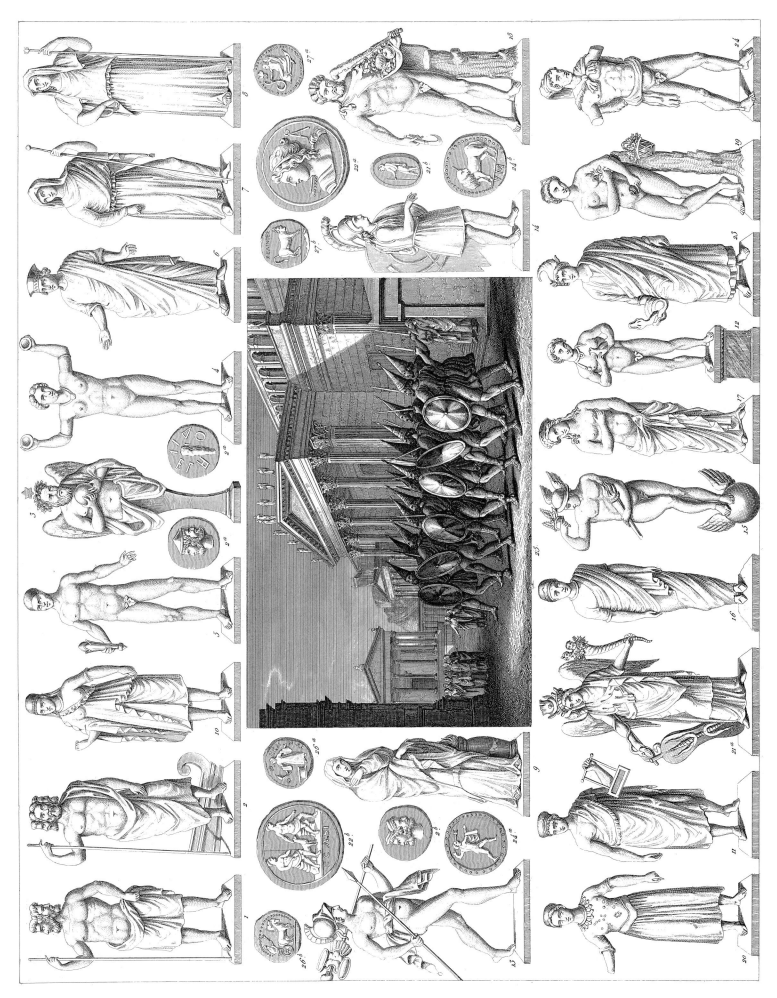

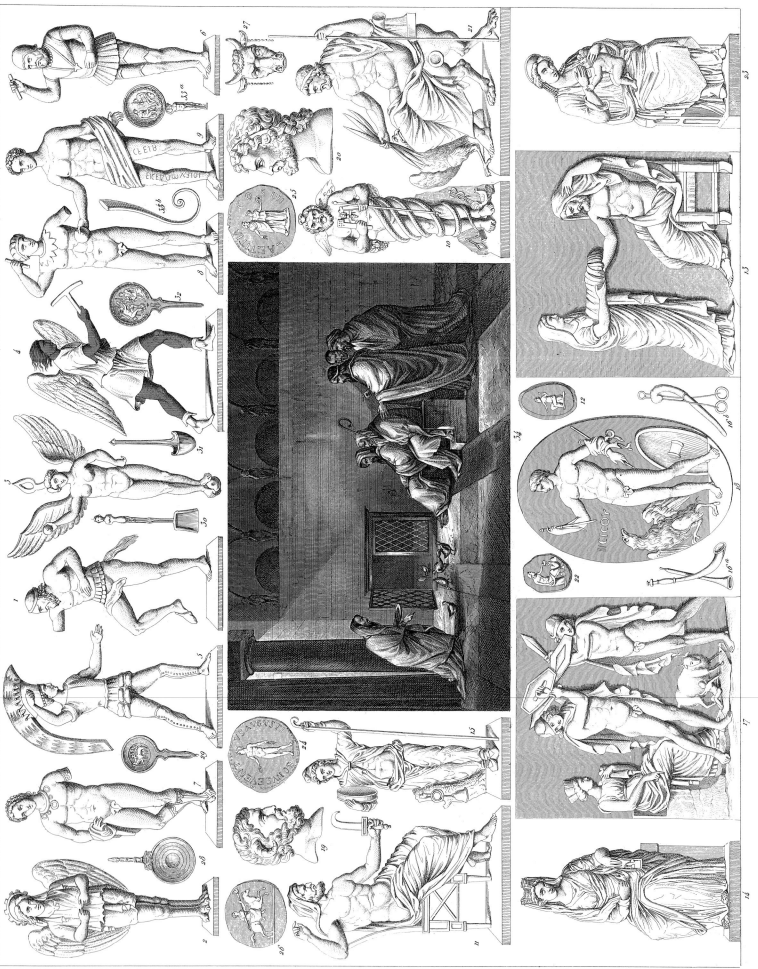

Mythology, Plate 16

76

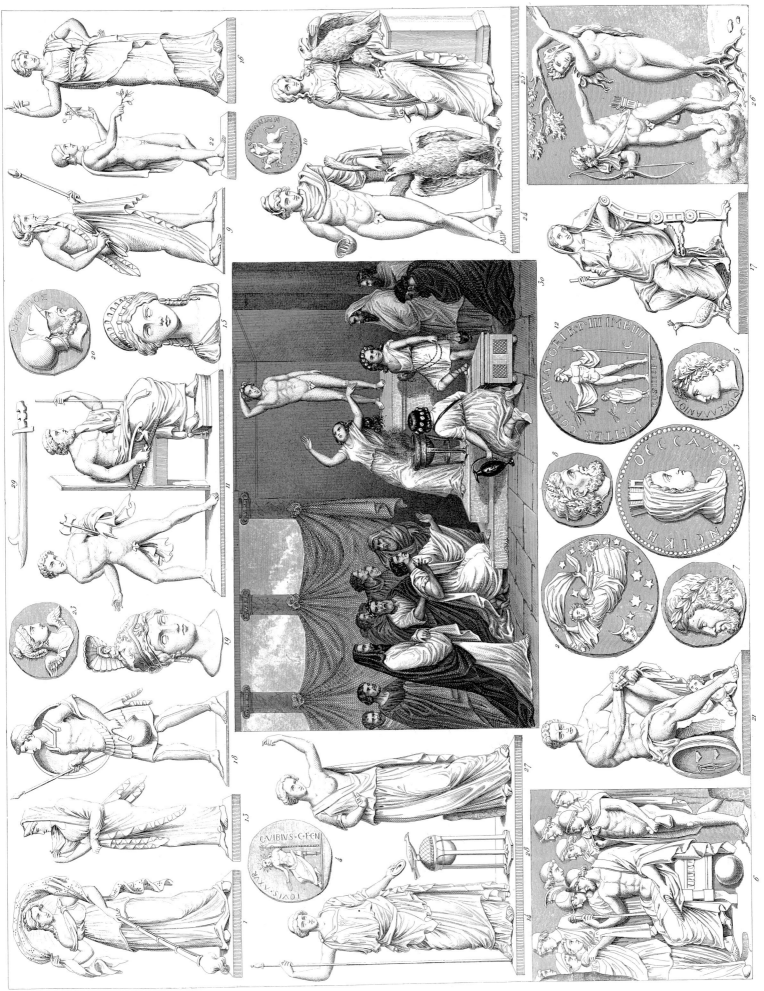

Mythology, Plate 17

77

Mythology, Plate 18

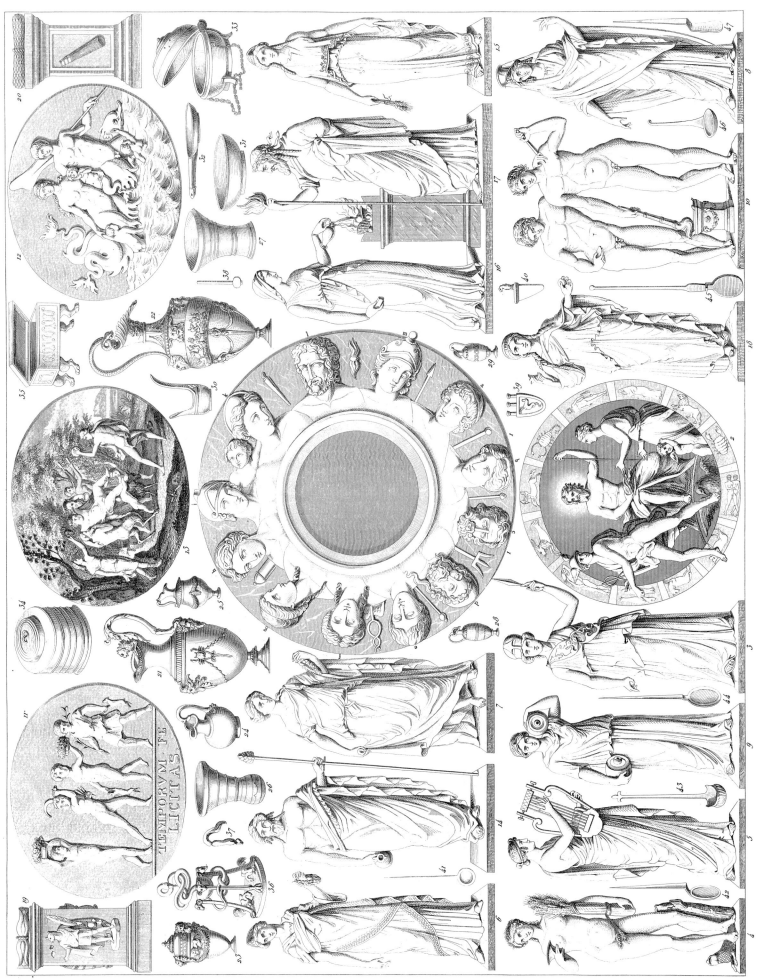

Mythology, Plate 19

79

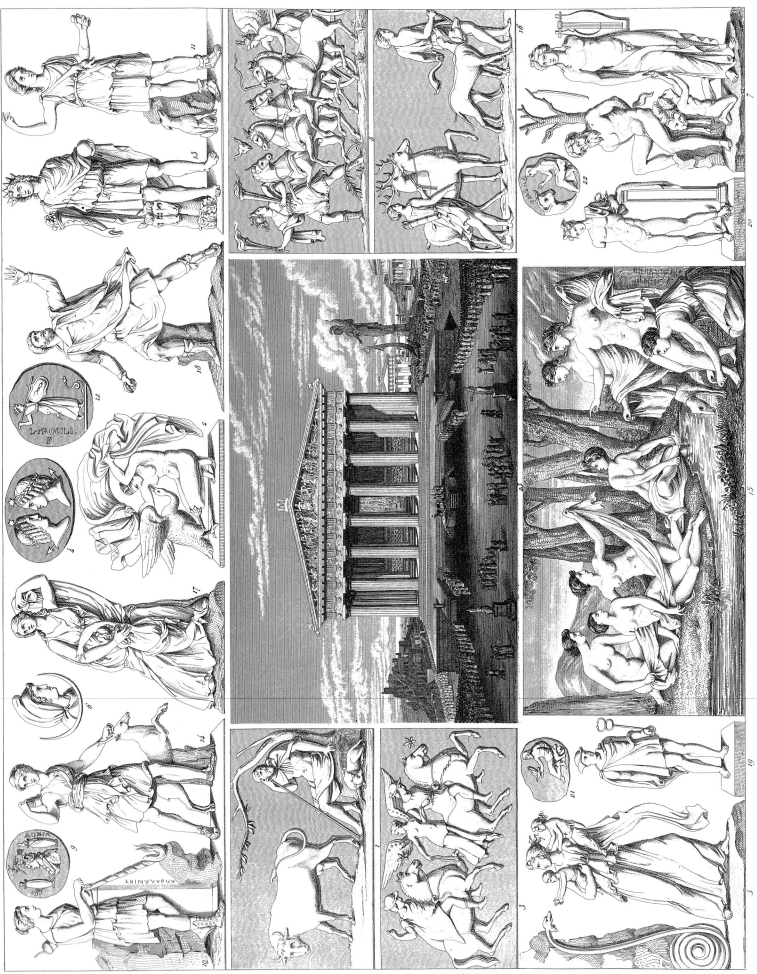

Mythology, Plate 20

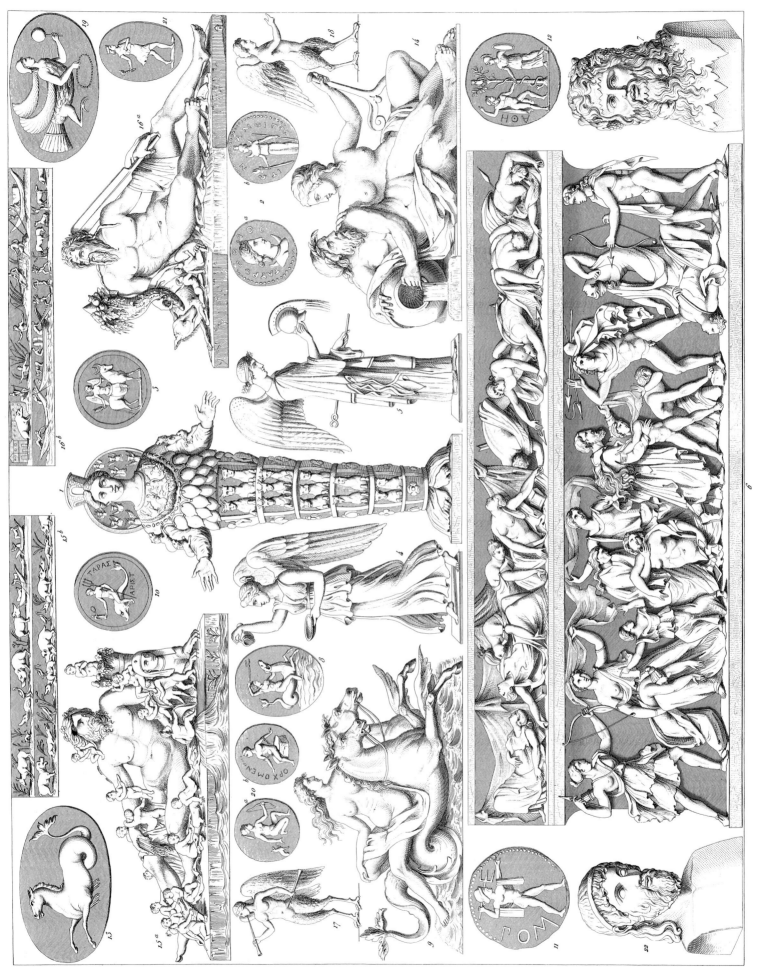

Mythology, Plate 21

81

Mythology, Plate 22

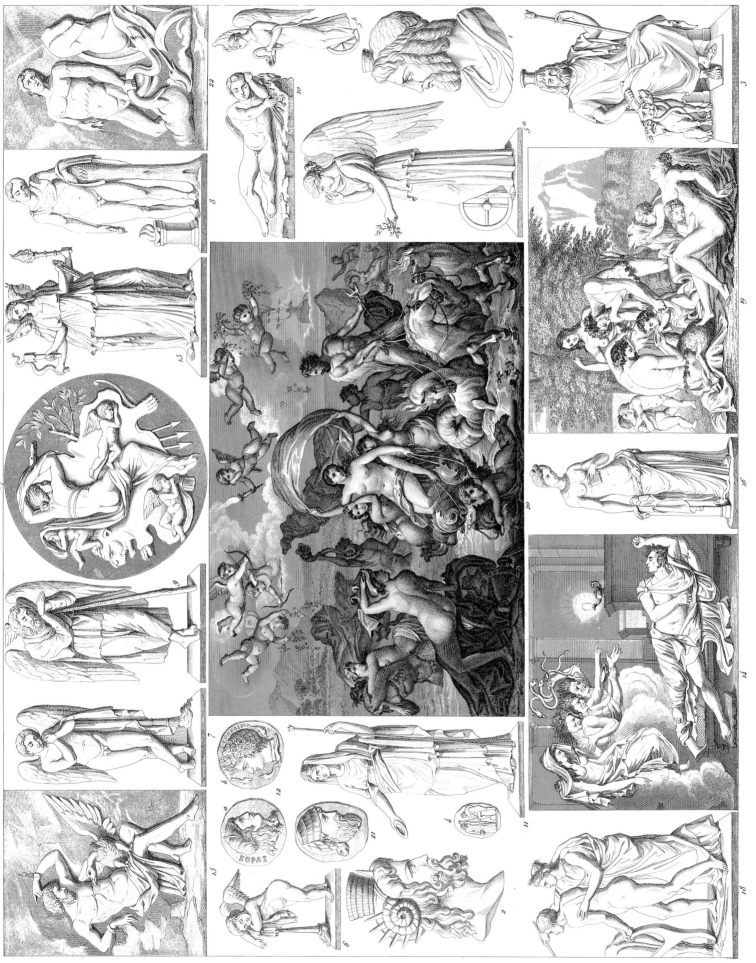

Mythology, Plate 23

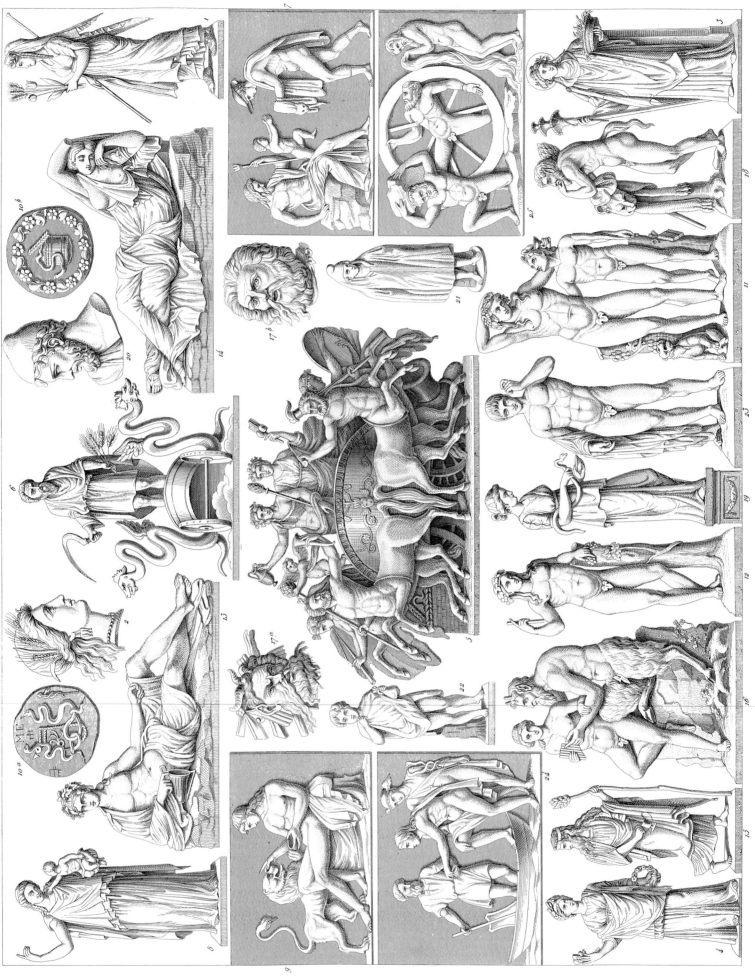

Mythology, Plate 24

84

Mythology, Plate 25

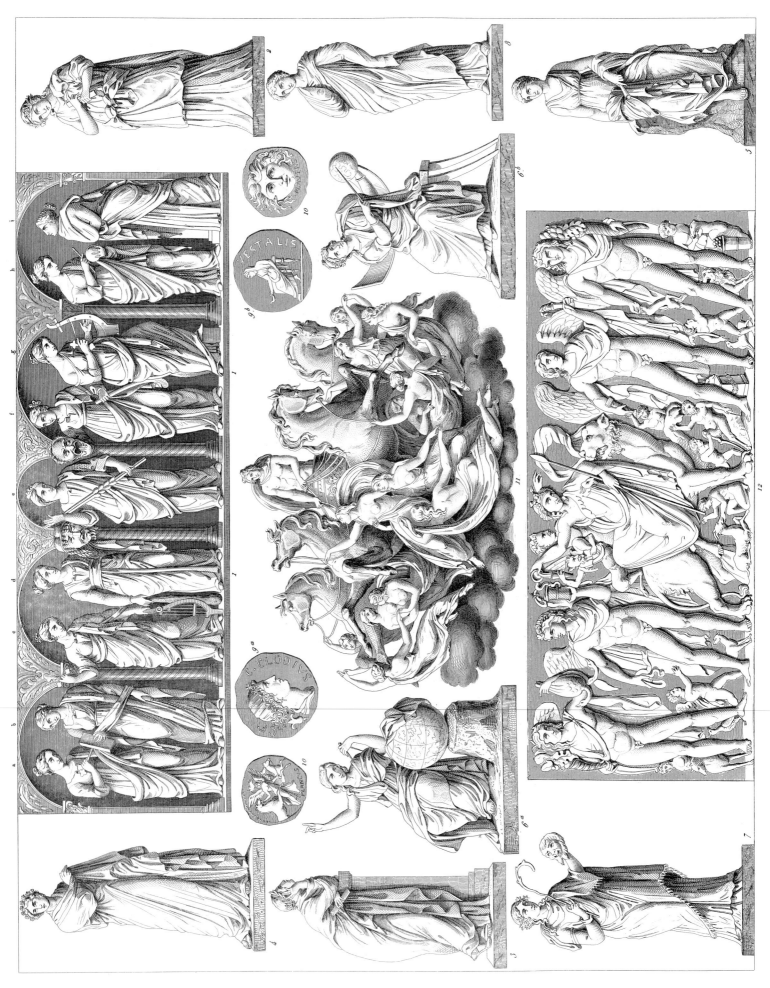

Mythology, Plate 26

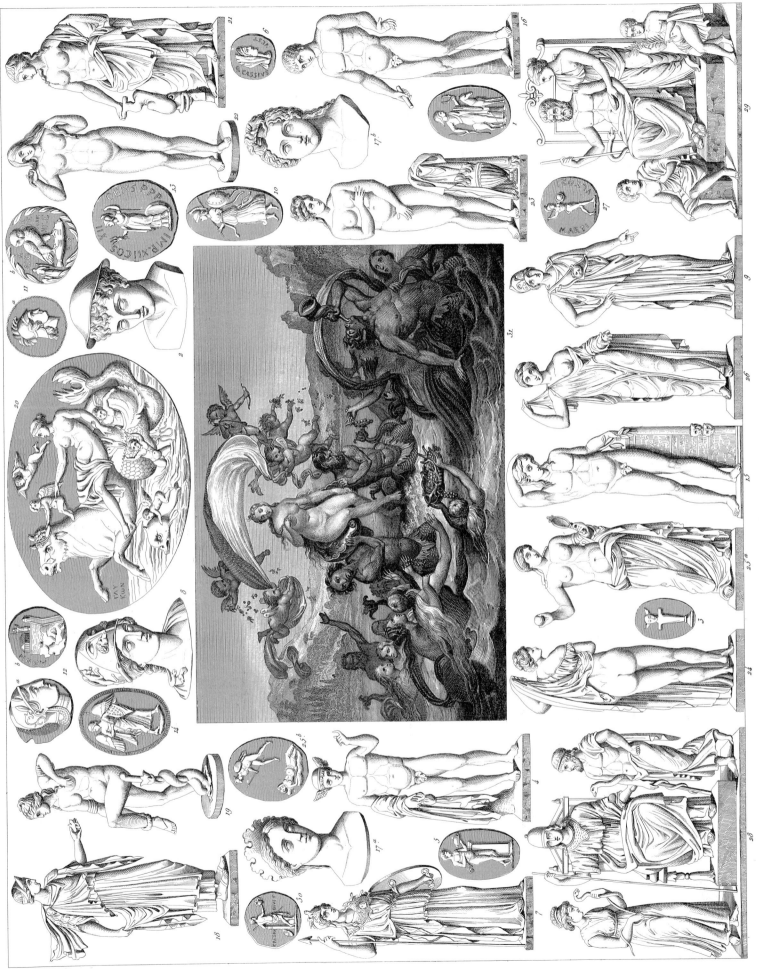

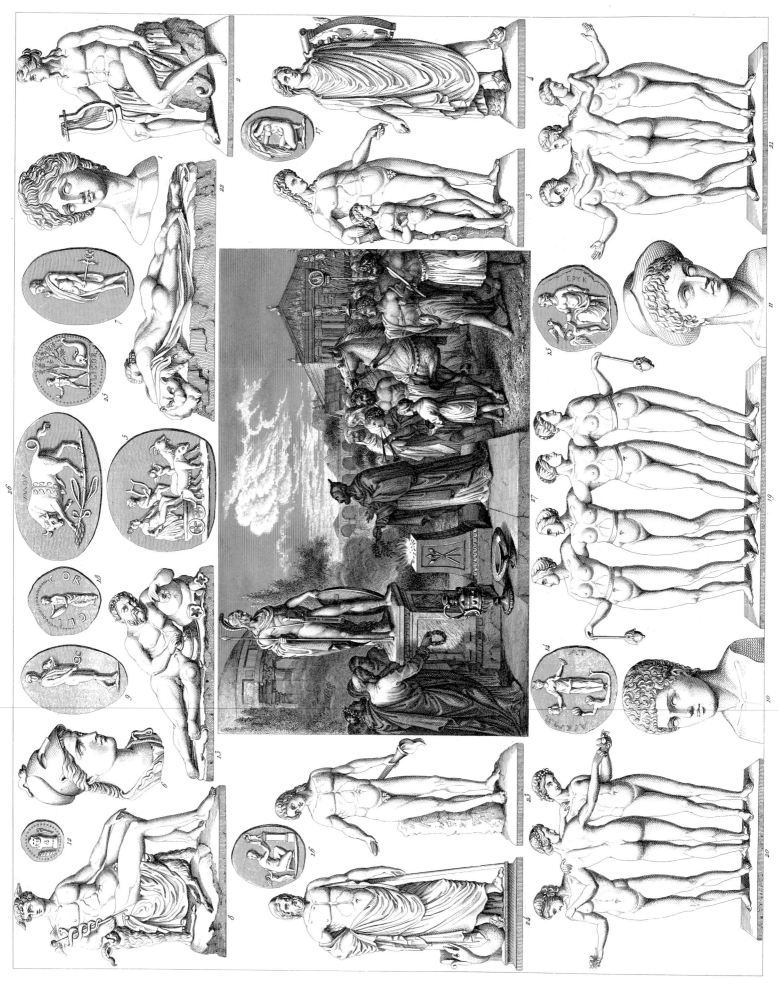

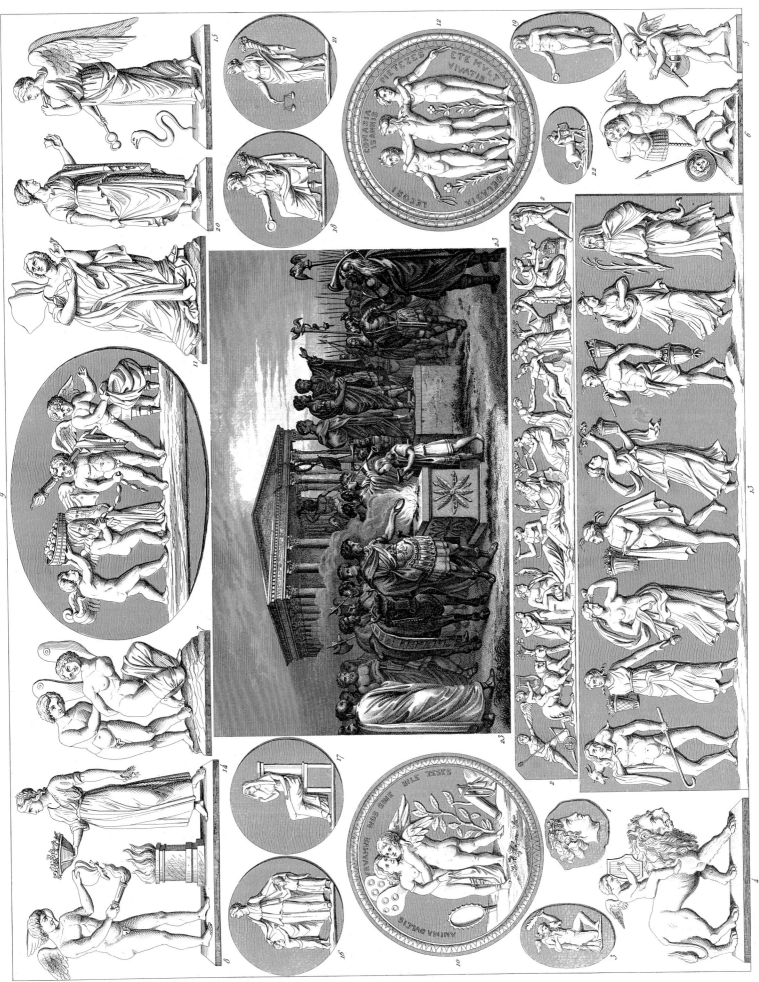

Mythology, Plate 29

89

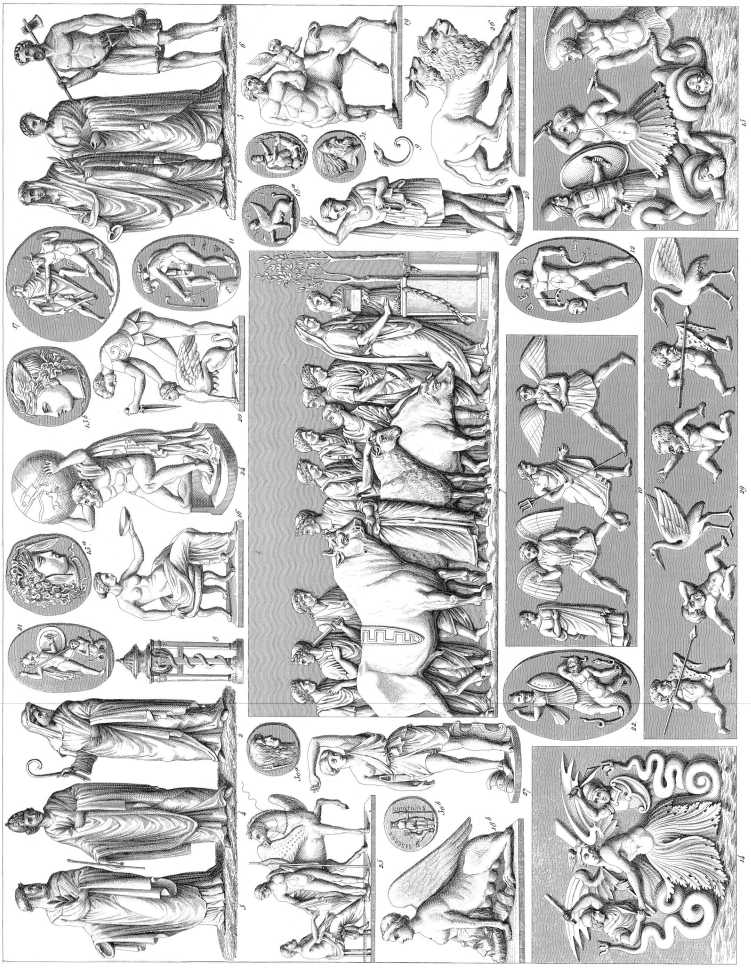

Mythology, Plate 30

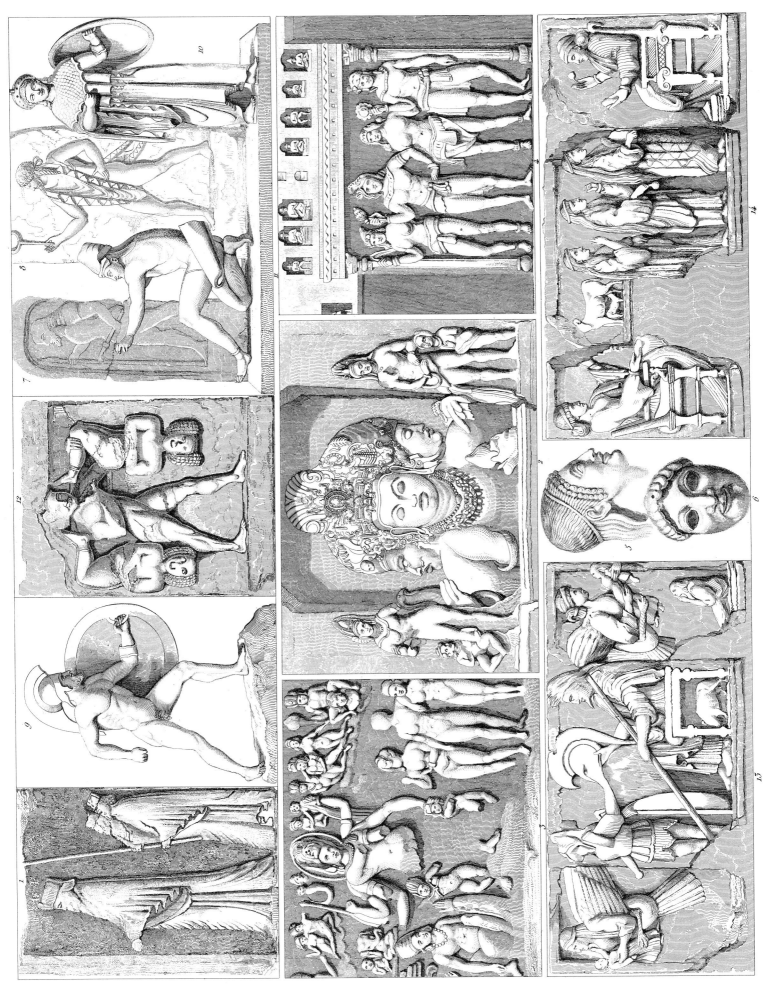

Fine Arts, Plate 1

91

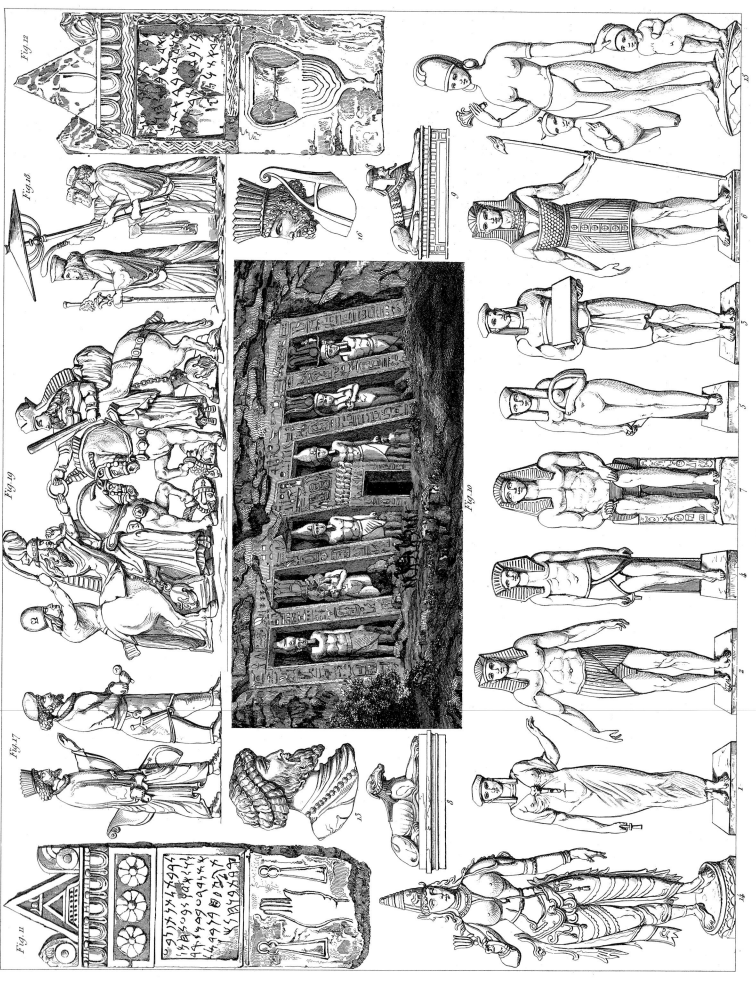

Fine Arts, Plate 2

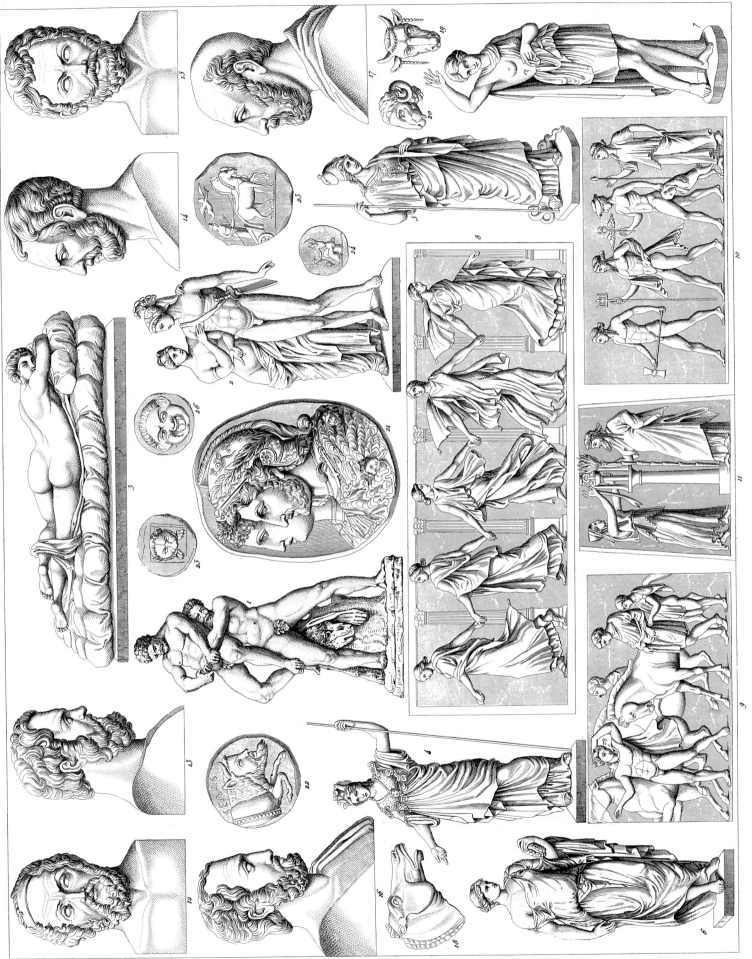

Fine Arts, Plate 3

93

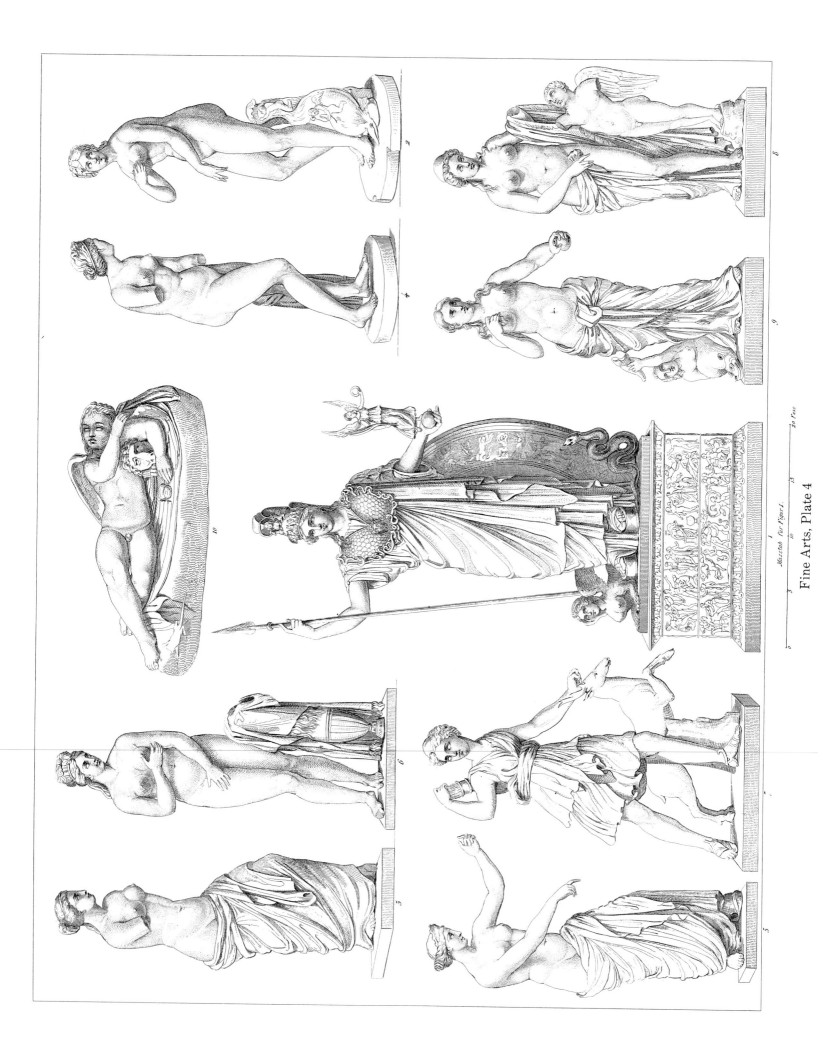

Fine Arts, Plate 4

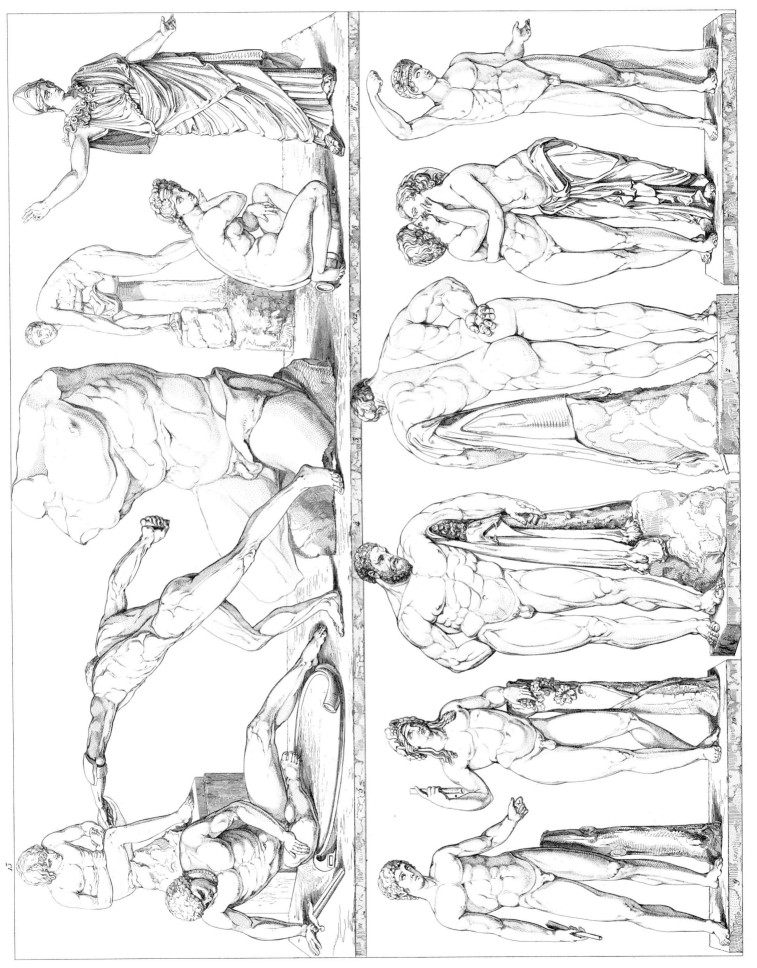

Fine Arts, Plate 5

95

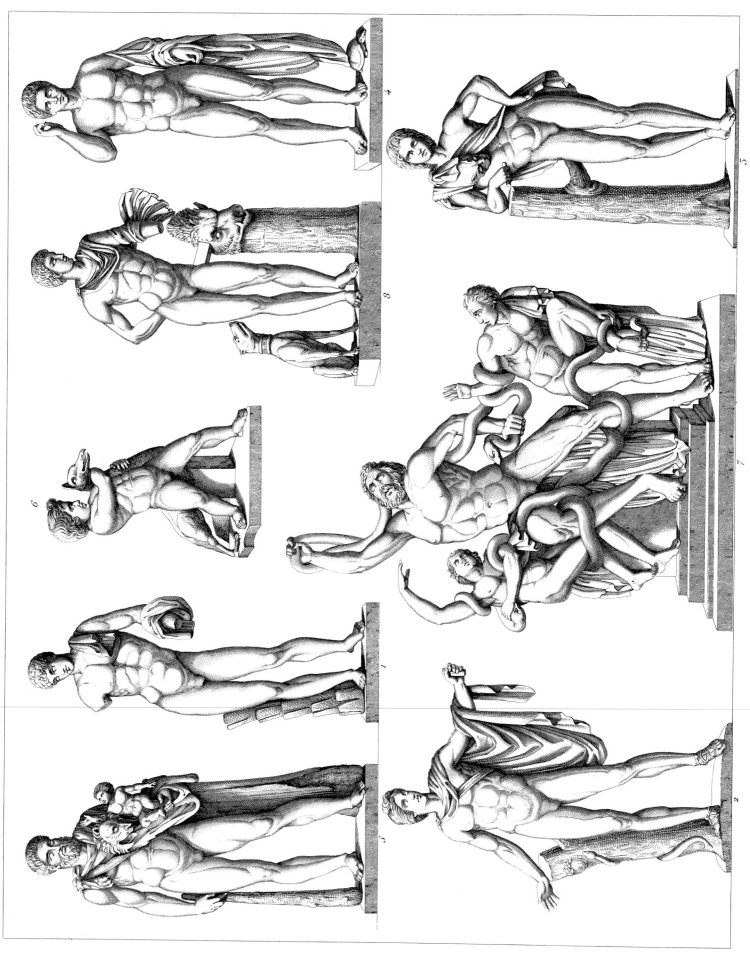

Fine Arts, Plate 6

96

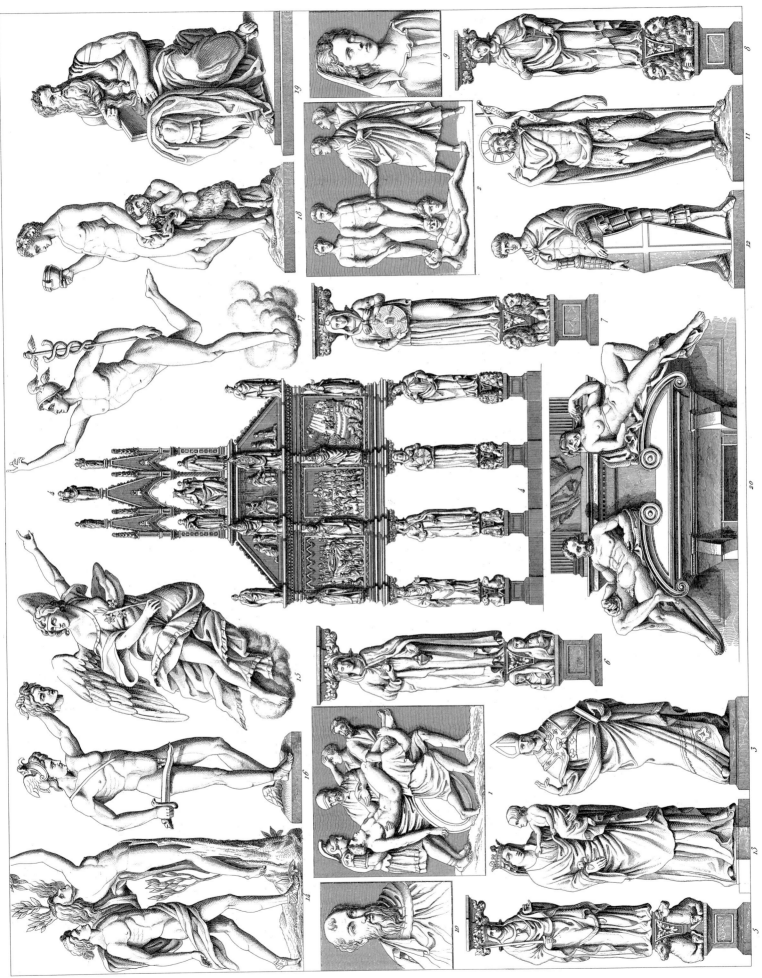

Fine Arts, Plate 7

97

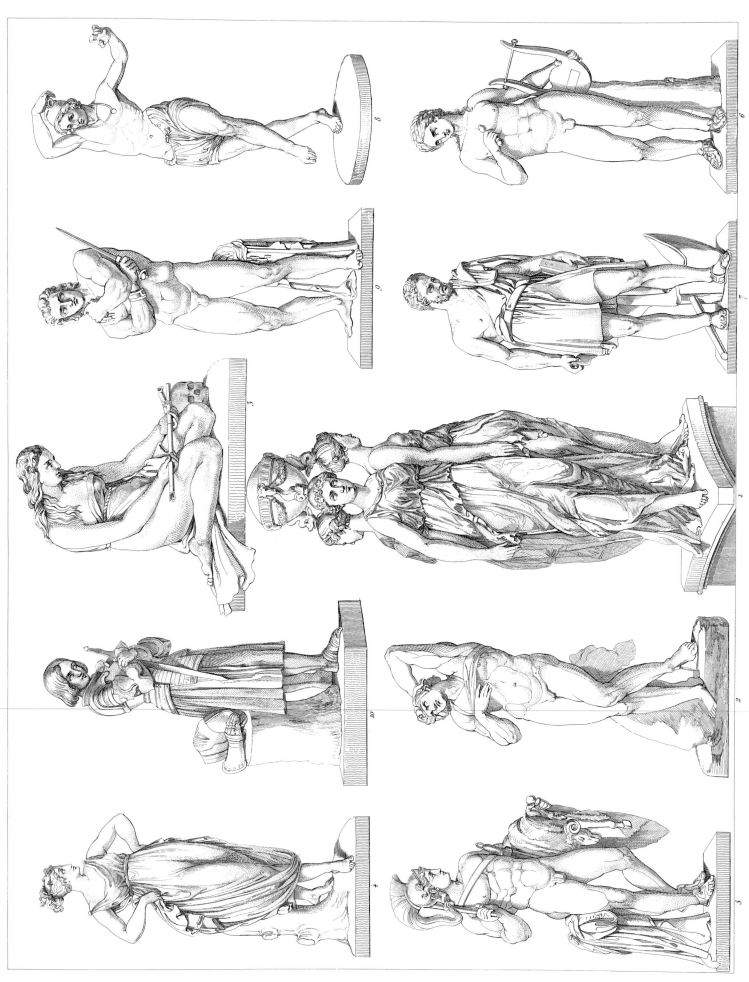

Fine Arts, Plate 8

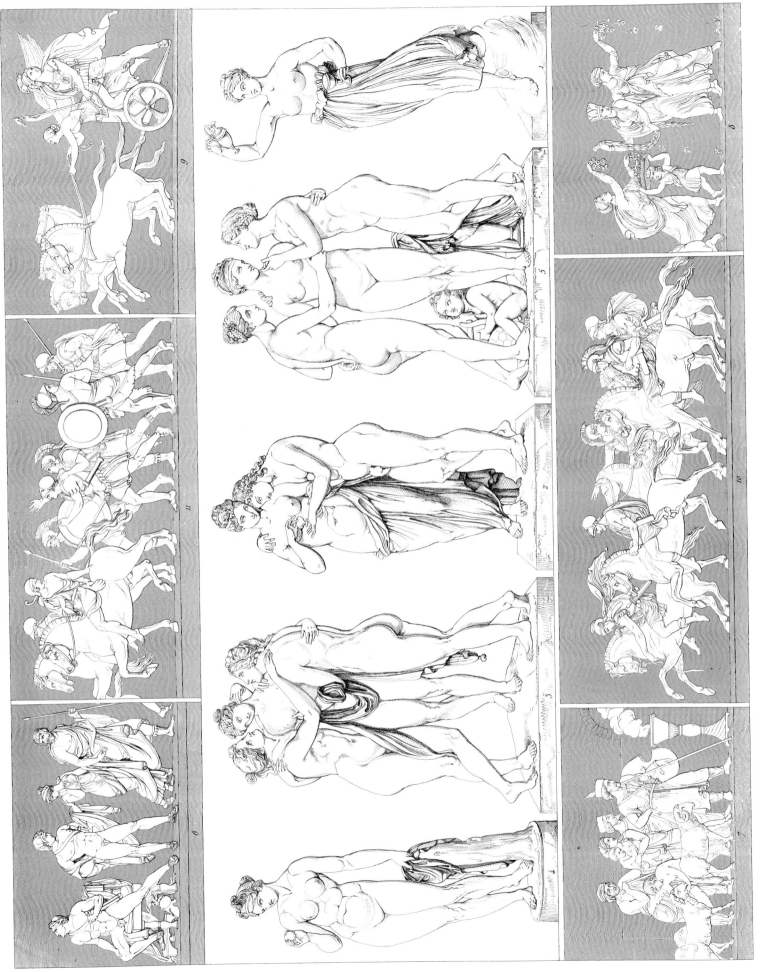

Fine Arts, Plate 9

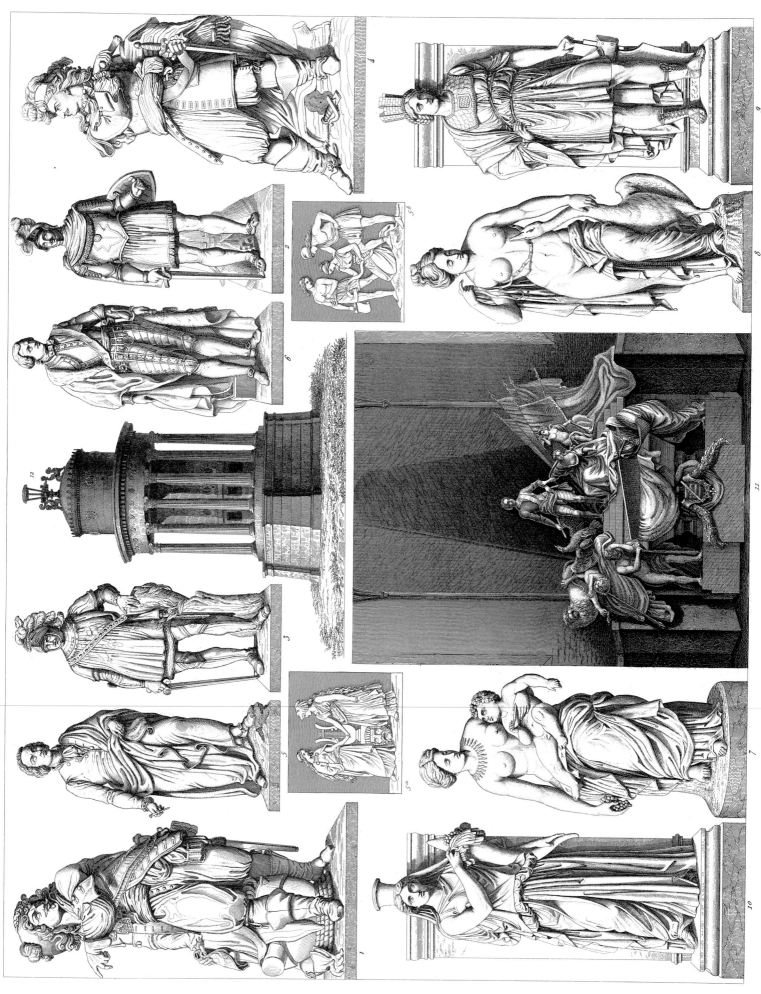

Fine Arts, Plate 10

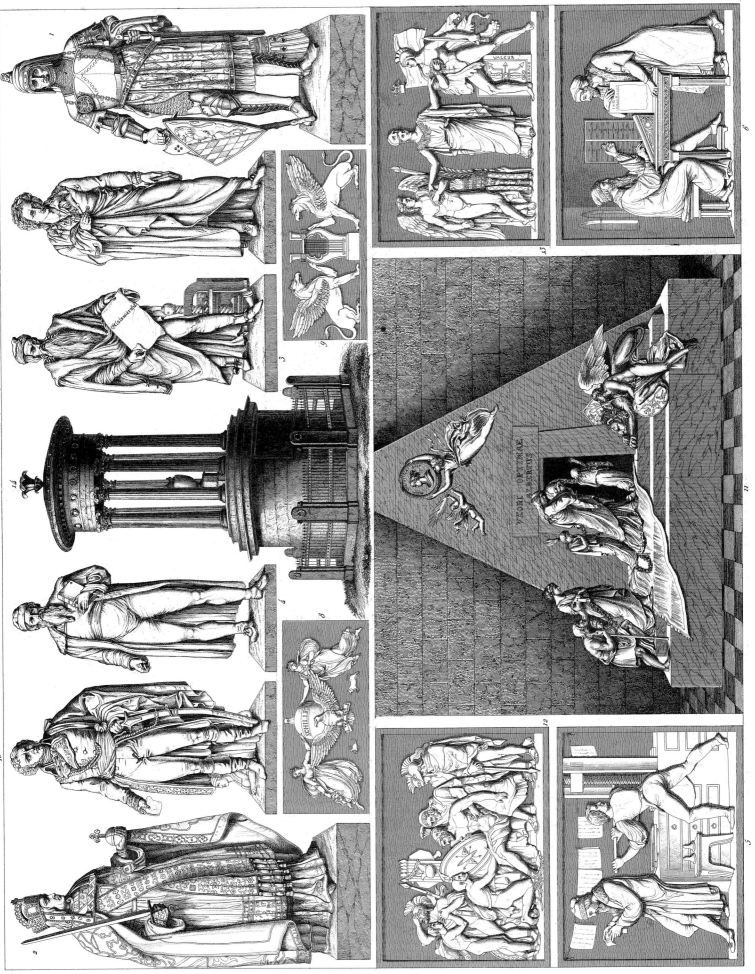

101

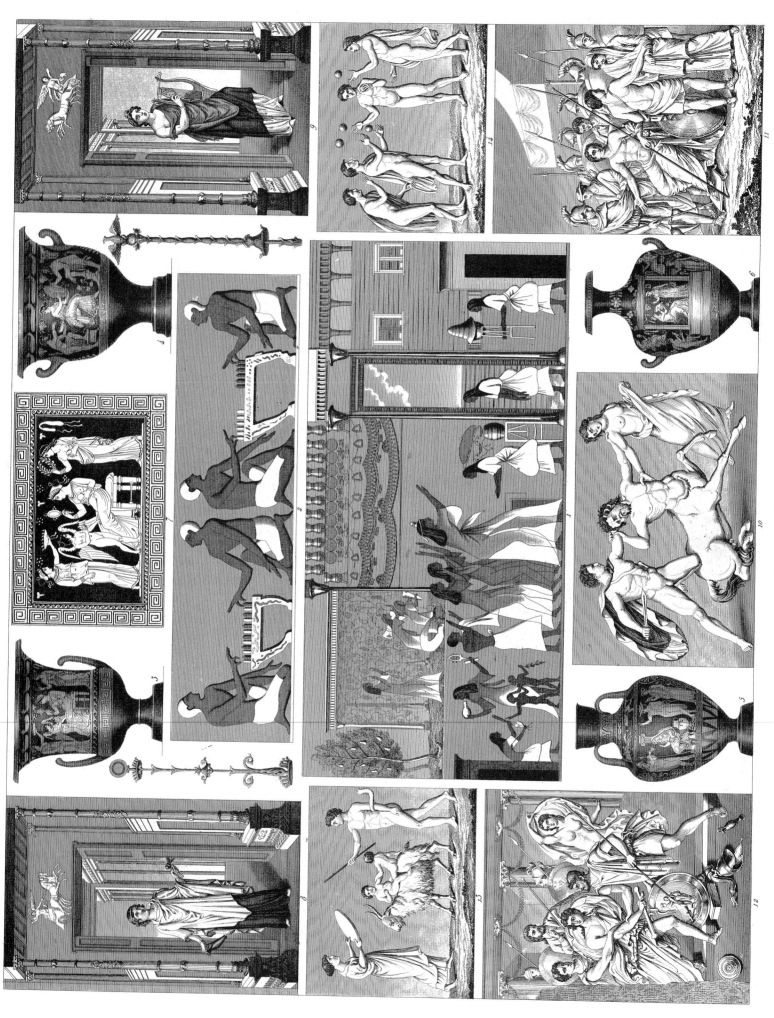

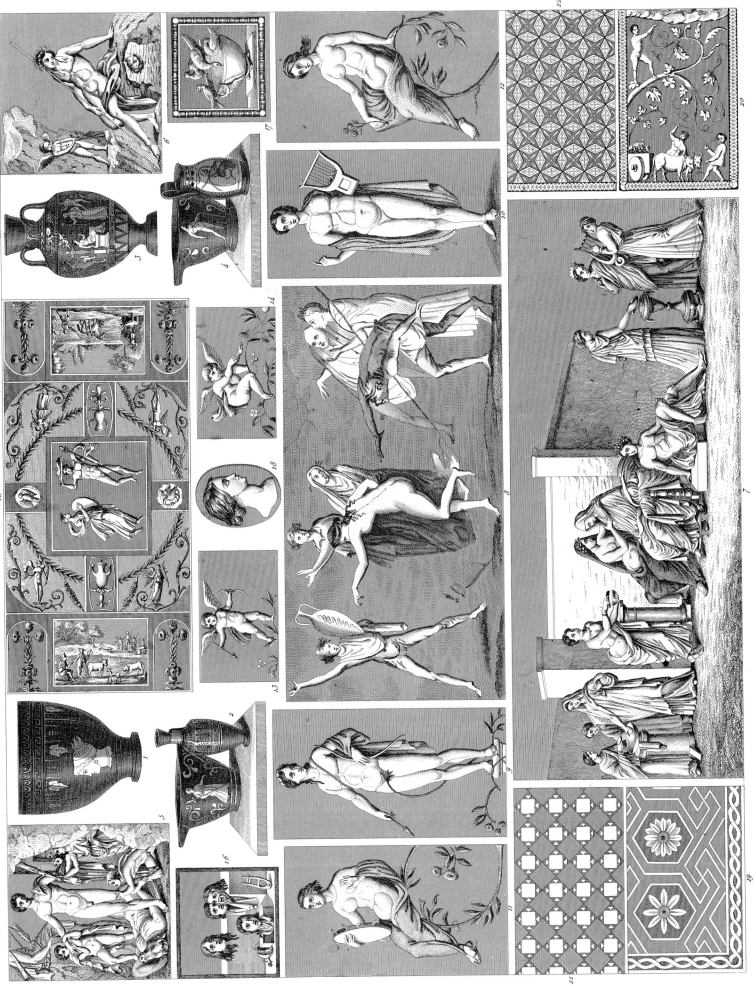

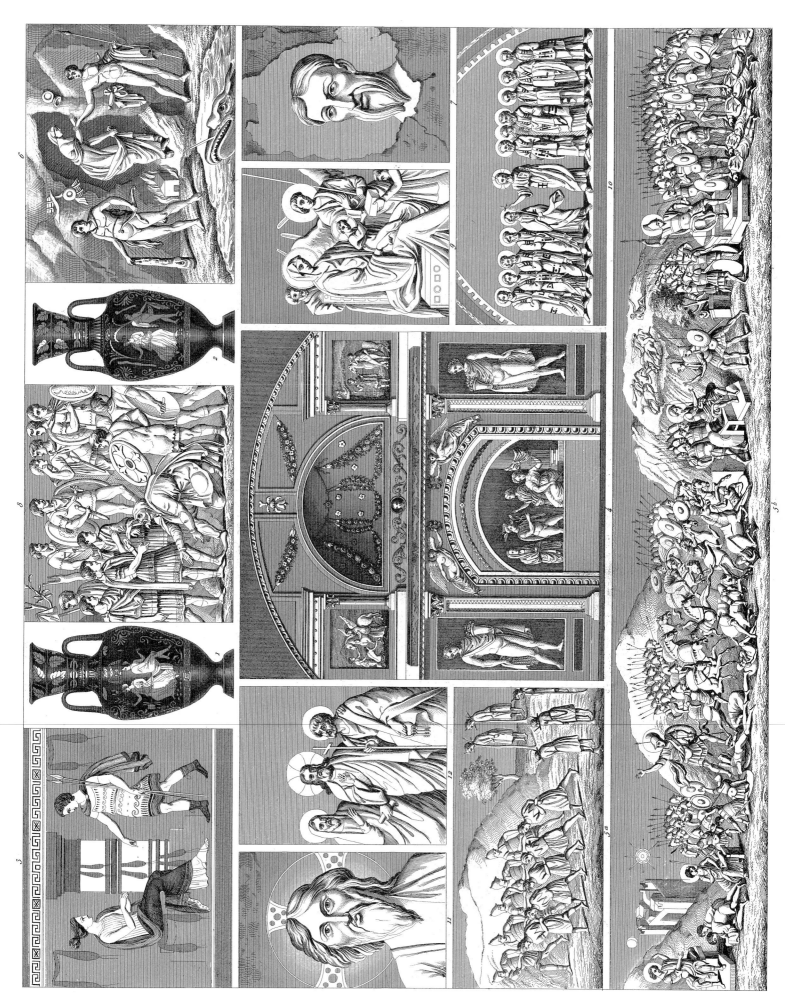

Fine Arts, Plate 14

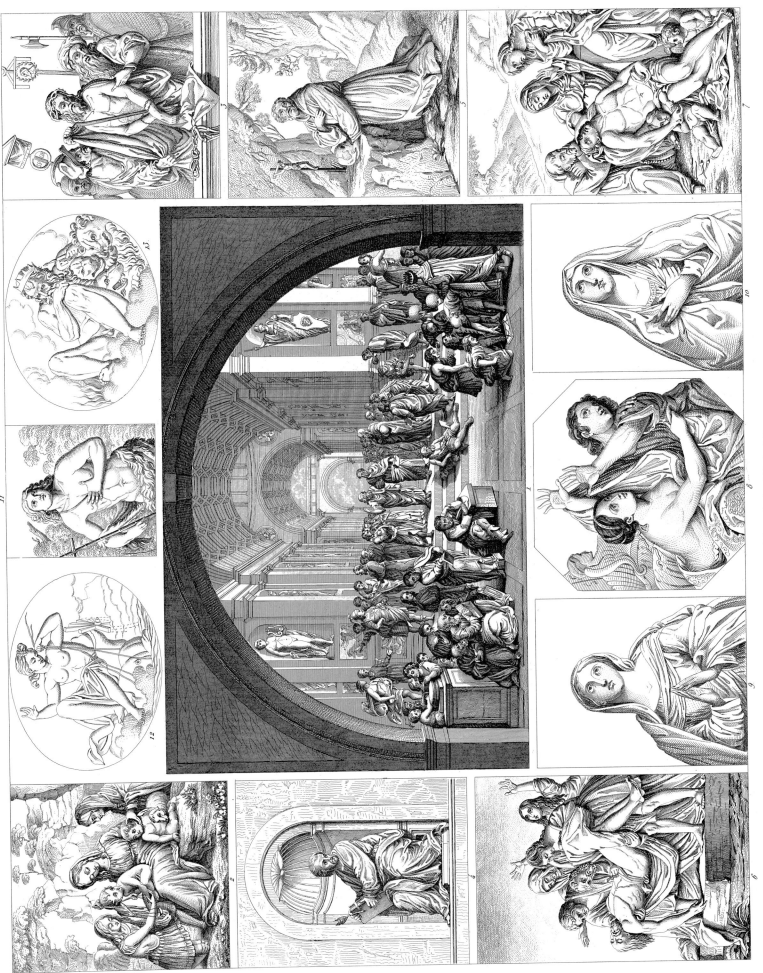

Fine Arts, Plate 15

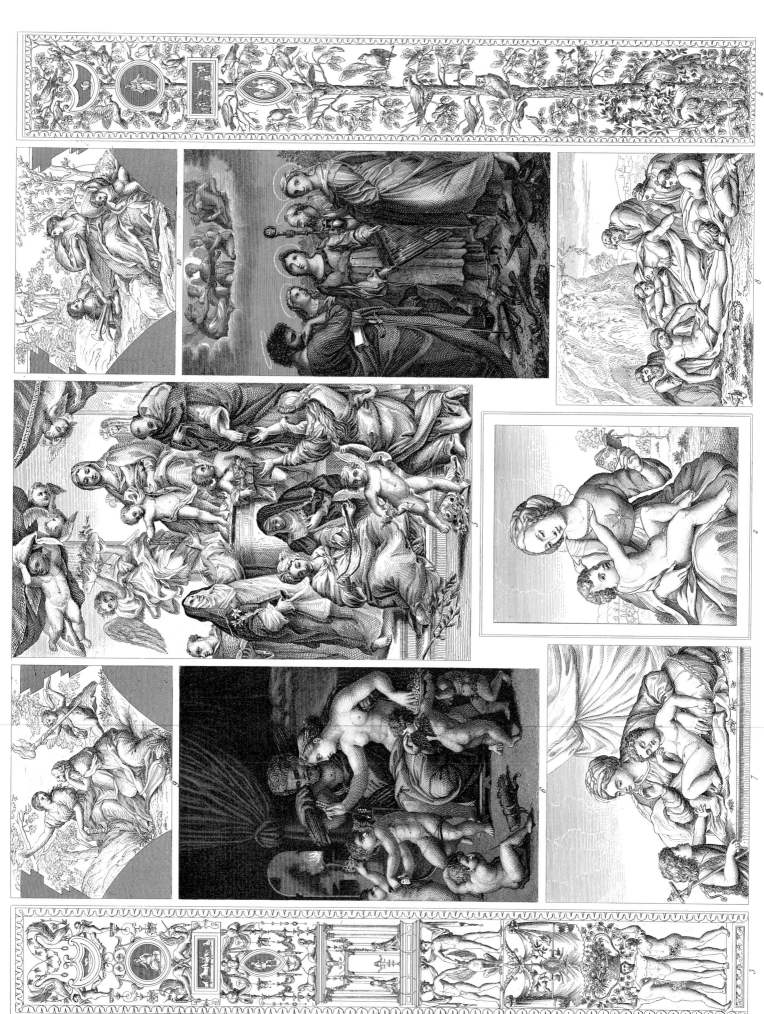

Fine Arts, Plate 16

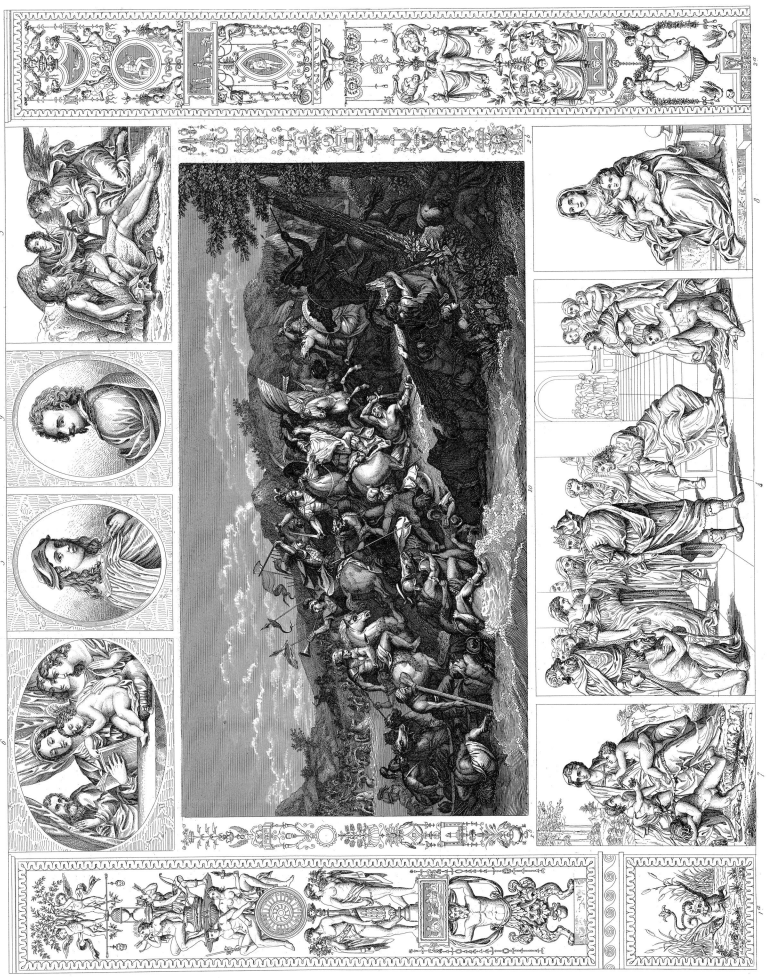

Fine Arts, Plate 17

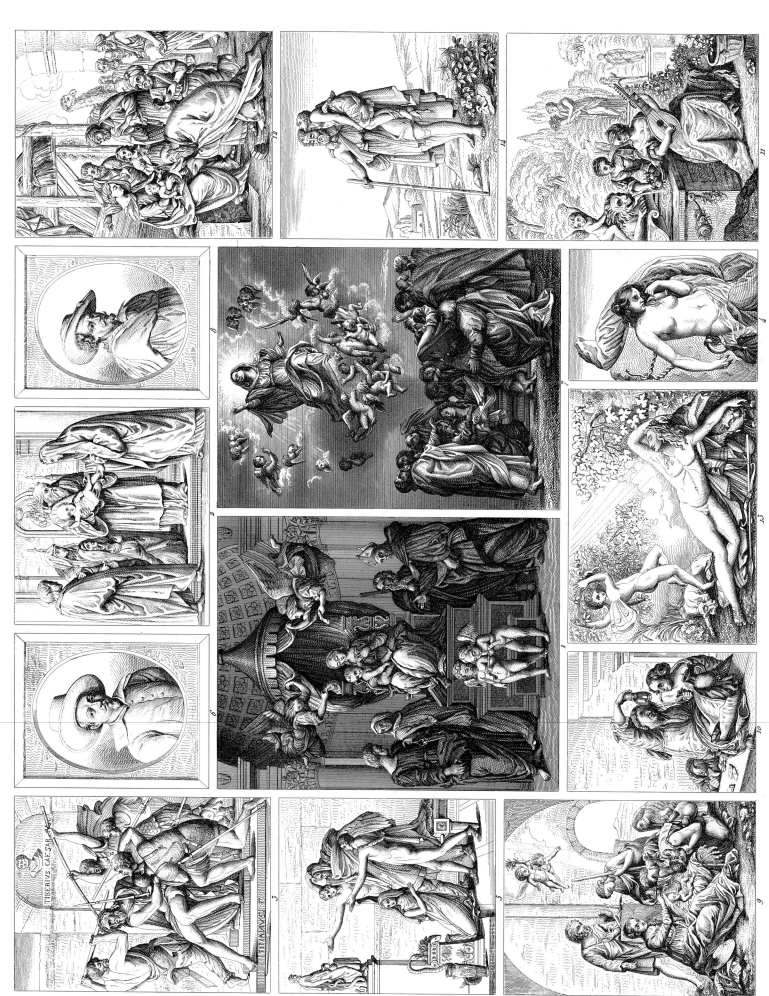

Fine Arts, Plate 18

108

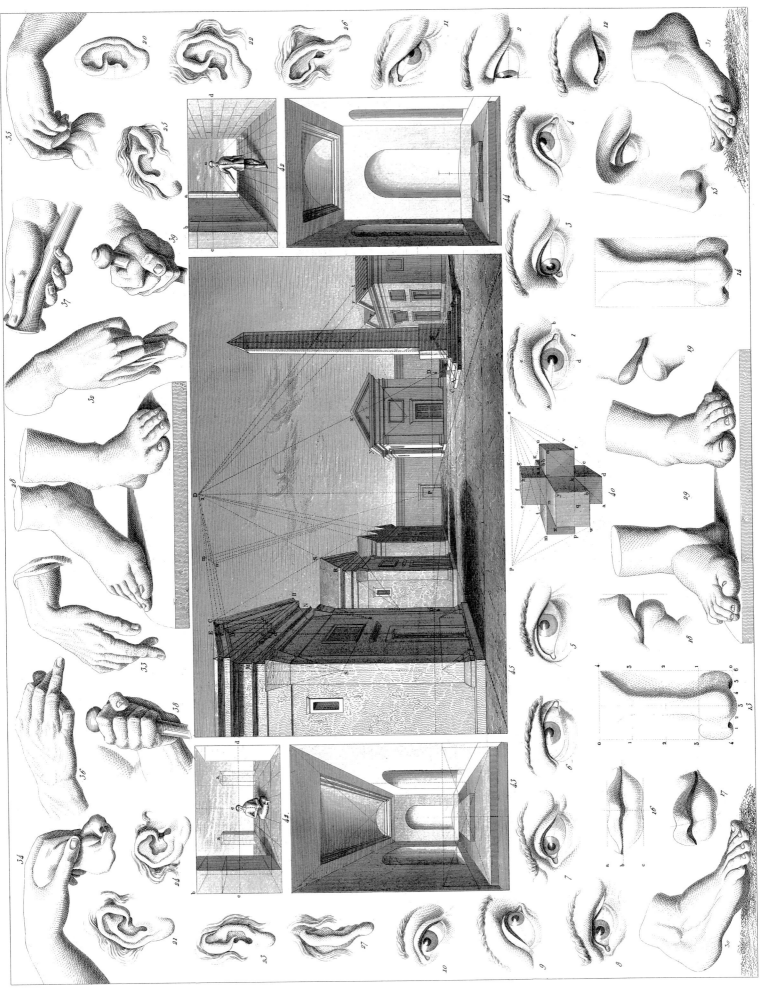

Fine Arts, Plate 19

109

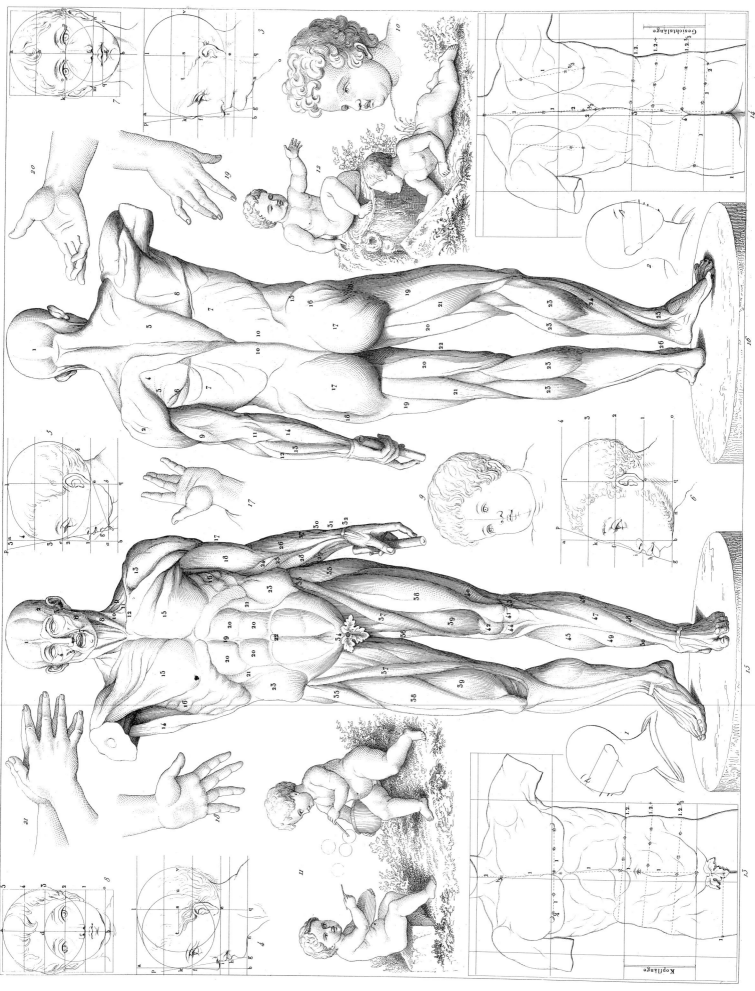

Fine Arts, Plate 20

Fine Arts, Plate 21

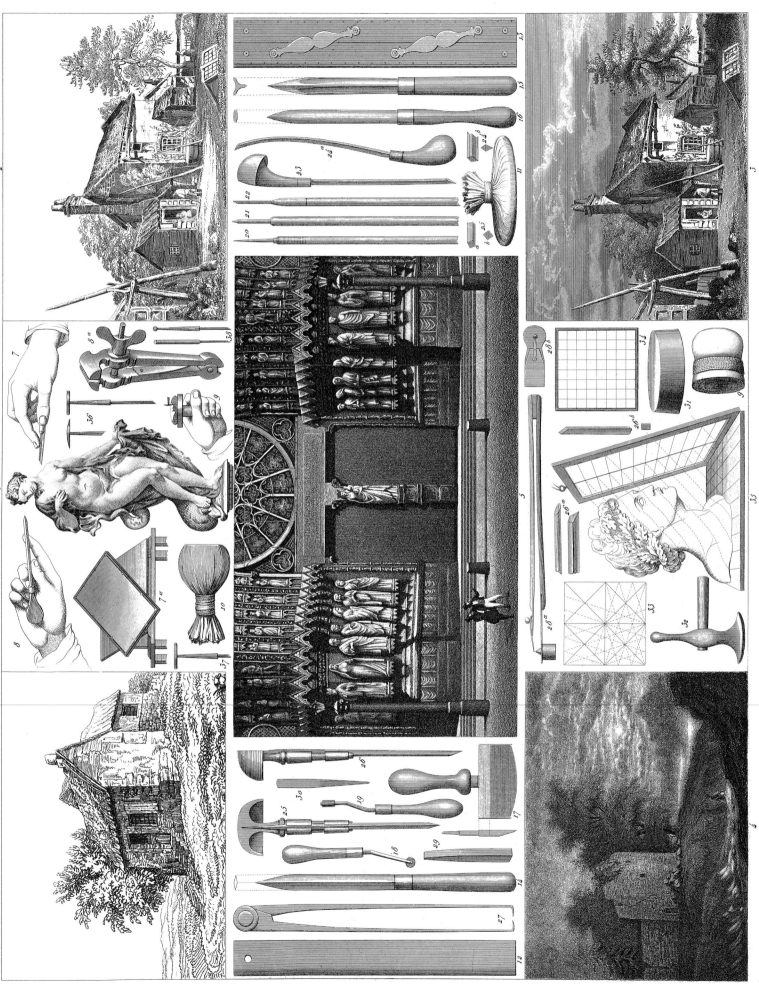

Fine Arts, Plate 22

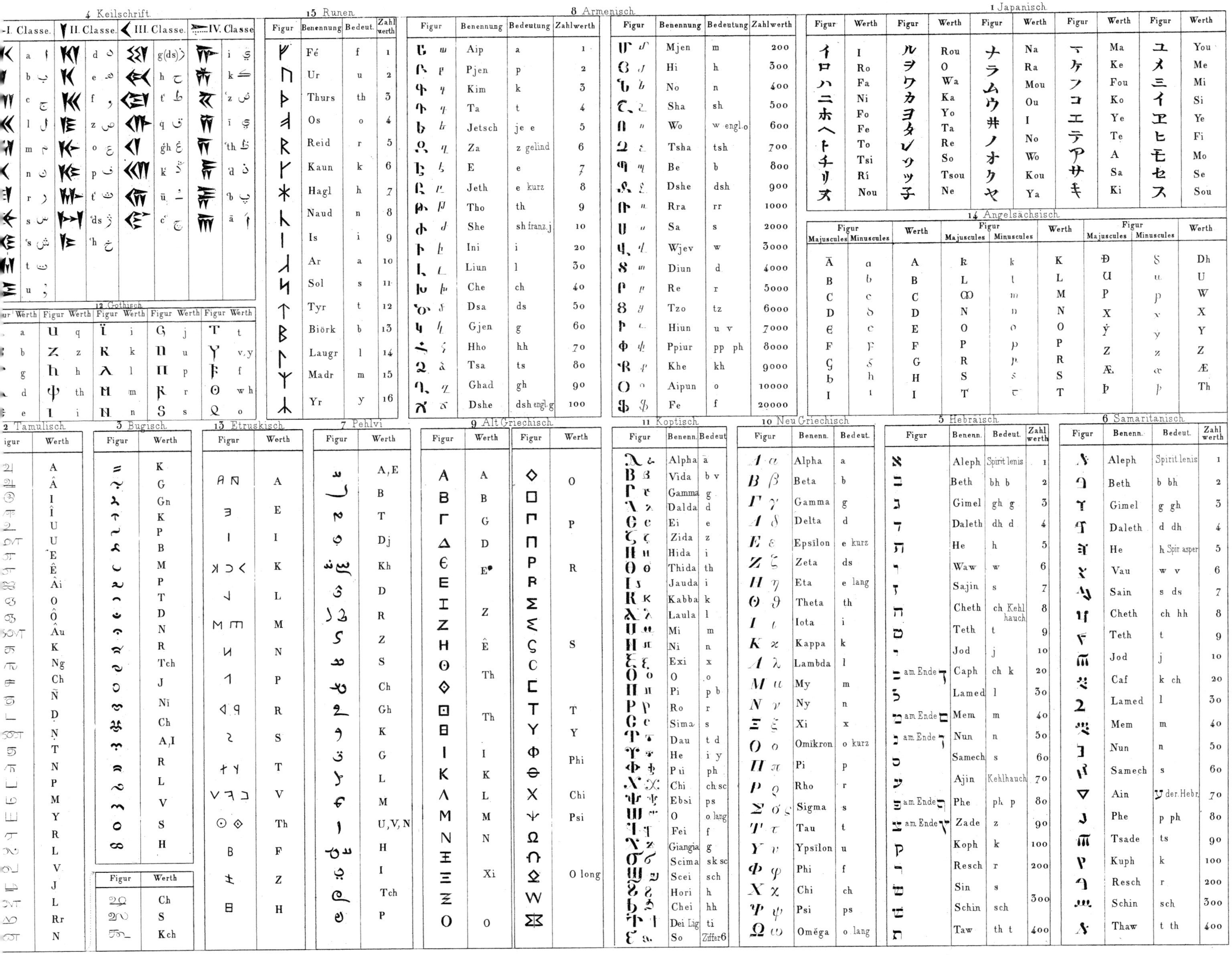

1 Japanisch

14 Angelsächsisch

6 Samaritanisch

5 Hebräisch

8 Armenisch

10 Neu Griechisch

11 Koptisch

9 Alt Griechisch

7 Pehlvi

4 Keilschrift

12 Gothisch

15 Runen

13 Etruskisch

3 Bugisch

2 Tamulisch

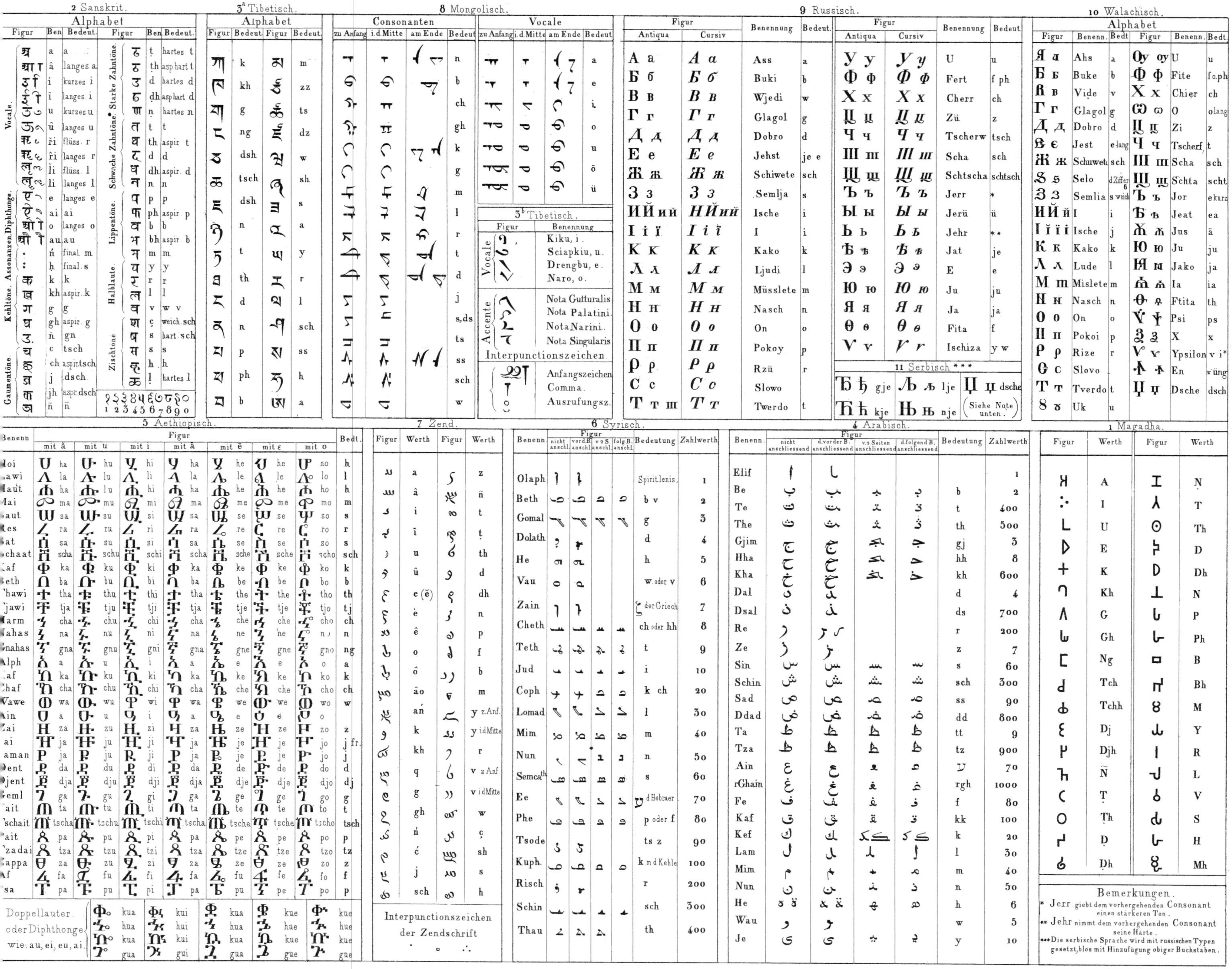

Fine Arts, Plate 24

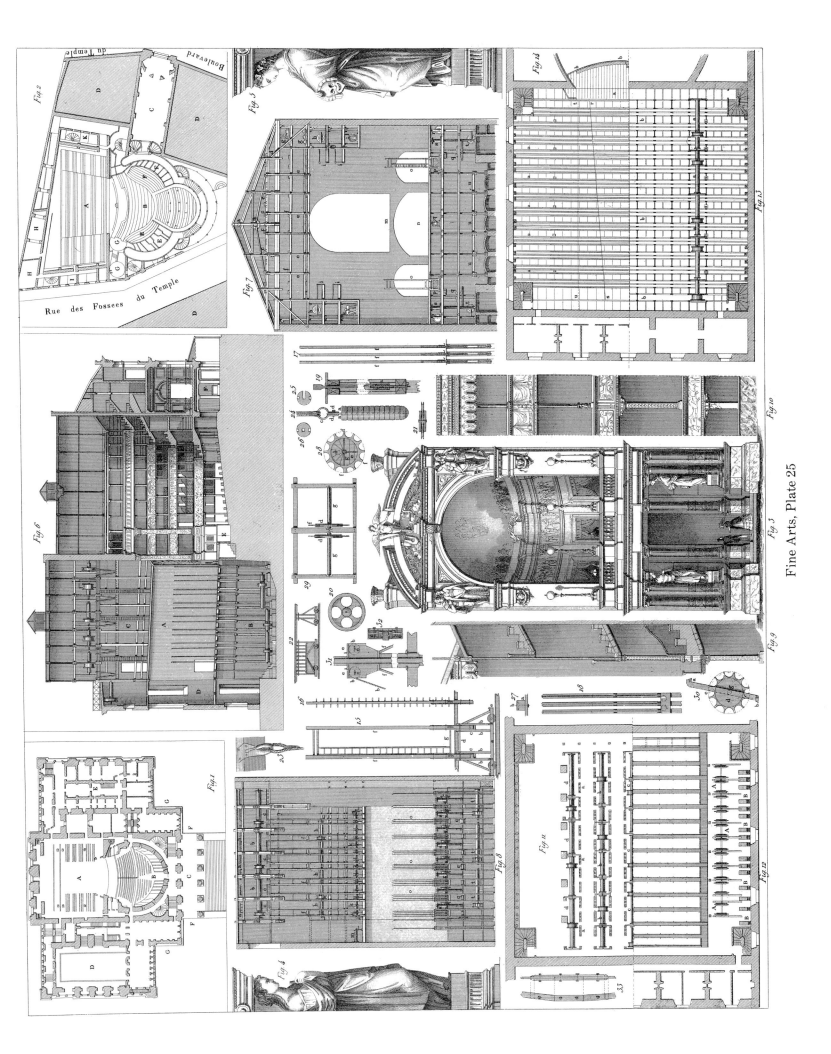

Fine Arts, Plate 25

115

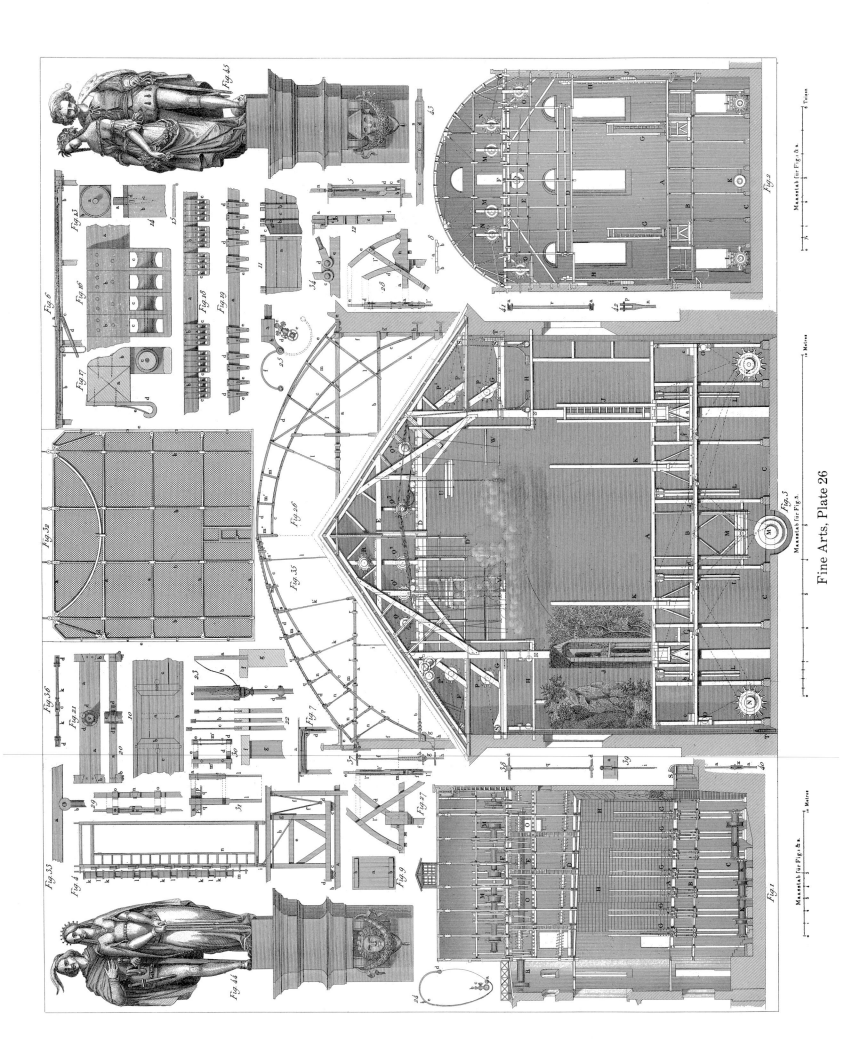

Fine Arts, Plate 26